THE ADDING MACHINE

THE
ADDING
MACHINE

SELECTED ESSAYS

William S. Burroughs

Seaver Books
New York

First published in the United States in 1986 by
Seaver Books, 333 Central Park West,
New York, New York 10025.
Published simultaneously in Canada.
Distributed in the United States by
Henry Holt and Company, 521 Fifth Avenue,
New York, New York 10175.
Originally published in Great Britain
under the title *The Adding Machine:
Collected Essays*.

Library of Congress Cataloging-in-Publication Data
Burroughs, William S., 1914–
The adding machine.
I. Title.
PS3552.U75A63   1986   814'.54   86-3765
ISBN 0-8050-0000-3

First American Edition

Printed in the United States of America
1 3 5 7 9 10 8 6 4 2

ISBN 0-8050-0000-3

Contents

THE ADDING MACHINE

The Name Is Burroughs

The name is Bill Burroughs. I am a writer. Let me tell you a few things about my job, what an assignment is like.

You hit Interzone with that grey anonymously ill-intentioned look all writers have.

'You crazy or something walk around alone? Me good guide. What you want Meester?'

'Well uh, I would like to write a bestseller that would be a good book, a book about real people and places . . .'

The Guide stopped me. 'That's enough Mister. I don't want to read your stinking book. That's a job for the White Reader.' The guide's face was a grey screen, hustler faces moved across it. 'Your case is difficult frankly. If we put it through channels they will want a big piece in advance. Now I happen to know the best continuity man in the industry, only handles boys he likes. He'll want a piece of you too but he's willing to take it on spec.'

People ask what would lead me to write a book like *Naked Lunch*. One is slowly led along to write a book and this looked good, no trouble with the cast at all and that's half the battle when you can find your characters. The more far-out sex pieces I was just writing for my own amusement. I would put them away in an old attic trunk and leave them for a distant boy to find . . . 'Why Ma this stuff is terrific — and I thought he was just an old book-of-the-month-club corn ball.'

Yes I was writing my bestseller . . . I finished it with a flourish, fading streets a distant sky, handed it to the publisher and stood there expectantly.

He averted his face . . . 'I'll let you know later, come around, in fact. Always like to see a writer's digs.' He coughed, as if he found my presence suffocating. A few nights later he visited me in my attic room, leaded glass windows under the slate roof. He did not remove his long black coat or his bowler hat. He dropped my manuscript on a table.

'What are you, a wise guy? We don't have a license on this.

1

The license alone costs more than we could clear.' His eyes darted around the room. 'What's that over there?' he demanded, pointing to a sea chest.

'It's a sea chest.'

'I can see that. What's in it?'

'Oh, nothing much, just some old things I wrote, not to show anybody, quite bad really . . .'

'Let's see some of it.'

Now, to say that I never intended publication of these pieces would not be altogether honest. They were there, just in case my bestseller fell on the average reader like a bag of sour dough — I've seen it happen, we all have: a book's got everything, topical my God, the scene is present-day Vietnam (Falkland Islands!) seen through a rich variety of characters . . . How can it miss? But it does. People just don't buy it. Some say you can put a curse on a book so the reader hates to touch it, or your book simply vanishes in a little swirl of disinterest. So I had to cover myself in case somebody had the curse in; after all, I am a professional. I like cool remote Sunday gardens set against a slate-blue mist, and for that set you need the Yankee dollar.

As a young child I wanted to be a writer because writers were rich and famous. They lounged around Singapore and Rangoon smoking opium in a yellow pongee silk suit. They sniffed cocaine in Mayfair and they penetrated forbidden swamps with a faithful native boy and lived in the native quarter of Tangier smoking hashish and languidly caressing a pet gazelle.

I can divide my literary production into sets: where, when and under what circumstances produced. The first set is a street of red brick three-story houses with slate roofs, lawns in front and large back yards. In our back yard my father and the gardener, Otto Belue, tended a garden with roses, peonies, iris and a fish pond. The address is 4664 Pershing Avenue and the house is still there.

My first literary endeavor was called 'The Autobiography of a Wolf', written after reading 'The Biography of a Grizzly Bear.' In the end this poor old bear, his health failing, deserted by his mate, goes to a valley he knows is full of poison gas. I can see a picture from the book quite clearly, a sepia valley, animal skeletons, the old bear slouching in, all the old broken voices from the family album find that valley where they come at last to die. 'They called me the Grey Ghost . . . Spent most of my time shaking off the ranchers.' The Grey Ghost met death at the hands of a grizzly bear after seven pages, no doubt in revenge for plagiarism.

There was something called *Carl Cranbury in Egypt* that never got off the ground . . . Carl Cranbury frozen back there on yellow lined paper, his hand an inch from his blue steel automatic. In this set I also wrote westerns, gangster stories, and haunted houses. I was quite sure that I wanted to be a writer.

When I was twelve we moved to a five-acre place on Price Road and I attended the John Burroughs School which is just down the road. This period was mostly crime and gangster stories. I was fascinated by gangsters and like most boys at that time I wanted to be one because I would feel so much safer with my loyal guns around me. I never quite found the sensitive old lady English teacher who molded my future career. I wrote at that time Edgar Allan Poe things, like old men in forgotten places, very flowery and sentimental too, that flavor of high school prose. I can taste it still, like chicken croquettes and canned peas in the school dining room. I wrote bloody westerns too, and would leave enigmatic skeletons lying around in barns for me to muse over . . .

'Tom was quick but Joe was quicker. He turned the gun on his unfaithful wife and then upon himself, fell dead in a pool of blood and lay there drawing flies. The vultures came later . . . especially the eyes were alike, a dead blue opaqueness.' I wrote a lot of hangings: 'Hardened old sinner that he was, he still experienced a shudder as he looked back at the three bodies twisting on ropes, etched against the beautiful red sunset.' These stories were read aloud in class. I remember one story written by another boy who later lost his mind, *dementia praecox* they called it: 'The captain tried to swim but the water was too deep and he went down screaming, "Help, help, I am drowning."'

And one story, oh very mysterious . . . an old man in his curtained nineteen-twenties Spanish library chances on a forgotten volume and there written in letters of gold the single word 'ATHENA.' . . . 'That question will haunt him until the house shall crumble to ruins and his books shall moulder away.'

At the age of fourteen I read a book called *You Can't Win*, being the life story of a second-story man. And I met the Johnson Family. A world of hobo jungles, usually by the river, where the bums and hobos and rod-riding pete men gathered to cook meals, drink canned heat, and shoot the snow . . . black smoke on the hip behind a Chink laundry in Montana. The Sanctimonious Kid: 'This is a crooked game, kid, but you have to think straight. Be as positive yourself as you like, but no positive clothes. You dress like every John Citizen or we part company, kid.' He was hanged in Australia for the murder of a constable.

And Salt Chunk Mary: 'Mary had all the no's and none of them ever meant yes. She received and did business in the kitchen. Mary kept an iron pot of salt chunk and a blue coffee pot always on the woodstove. You eat first and then you talk business, your gear slopped out on the kitchen table, her eyes old, unbluffed, unreadable. She named a price, heavy and cold as a cop's blackjack on a winter night. She didn't name another. She kept her money in a sugar bowl but nobody thought about that. Her cold grey eyes would have seen the thought and maybe something goes wrong on the next day, Johnny Law just happens by or Johnny Citizen comes up with a load of double-ought buckshot into your soft and tenders. It wouldn't pay to get gay with Mary. She was a saint to the Johnson Family, always good for a plate of salt chunk. One time Gimpy Gates, an old rod-riding pete man, killed a bum in a jungle for calling Salt Chunk Mary an old fat cow. The old yegg looked at him across the fire, his eyes cold as gunmetal . . . 'You were a good bum, but you're dogmeat now.' He fired three times. The bum fell forward, his hands clutching coals, and his hair catching fire. Well, the bulls pick up Gates and show him the body: 'There's the poor devil you killed, and you'll swing for it.' The old Yegg looked at them coldly. He held out his hand, gnarled from years of safe-cracking, two fingers blown off by the 'soup'. 'If I killed him, there's the finger pulled the trigger and there's the tendon pulled the finger.' The old yegg had beaten them at their own game.

This inspired me to write some crime stories . . . 'Here's to crime!' he shouted and raised a glass of champagne, but he crumpled like a pricked balloon as the heavy hand of Detective Sergeant Murphy fell on his shoulder.' . . . 'Joe Maguire regarded the flushed face of the dealer with disfavor. "A coke bird," he decided. "Better cut him off the payroll; get coked up and shoot a good client."'

I did a short story too, with a trick ending about this gangster who goes to a fortune-teller . . . 'This man is a criminal,' she thought shrewdly, 'a gangster, perhaps . . . he must have made enemies.' 'I see danger,' she said. The man's face twitched — he needed to snow. 'I see a man approaching . . . he has a gun . . . he lifts the gun . . . he —' With an inarticulate cry the man leapt to his feet and whipped out an automatic, spitting death at the fortune-teller . . . blood on the crystal ball, and on the table, a severed human hand.

After reading Eugene Aram's *Dream* — which I committed to memory and recited to the class in sepulchral tones — I wrote a series about murderers who all died of brain fever in a screaming delirium of remorse, and one character in the desert who murdered all his companions — sitting there looking at the dead bodies and wondering why he did it. When the vultures came and ate them he got so much relief he called them 'the vultures of gold' and that was the title of my story, *The Vultures of Gold*, which closed this rather nauseous period.

At fifteen I was sent to the Los Alamos Ranch School for my health, where they later made the first atom bomb. It seemed so right somehow, like the school song . . .

> '*Far away and high on the mesa's crest*
> *Here's the life that all of us love best*
> *Los Allll-amos.*'

Far away and high on the Mesa's crest I was forced to become a Boy Scout, eat everything on my plate, exercise before breakfast, sleep on a porch in zero weather, stay outside all afternoon, ride a sullen, spiteful, recalcitrant horse twice a week and all day on Saturday. We all had to become Boy Scouts and do three hours a week of something called C.W. — Community Work — which was always something vaguely unpleasant and quite useless too, but A.J. said it was each boy's cooperative contribution to the welfare and maintenance of the community. We had to stay outdoors, no matter what, all afternoon — they even timed you in the john. I was always cold, and hated my horse, a sulky strawberry roan. And the C.W. was always hanging over you. There were crew-leaders, you understand, many of them drunk with power — who made life hell for the crew.

This man had conjured up a whole city there. The school was entirely self-sufficient, raised all the food, etcetera. There was a store, a post office, and one of the teachers was even a magistrate. I remember once he got a case which involved shooting a deer out of season and he made the most of it, went on for days. He had founded the School after he quit the Forest Service because some inspirational woman told him 'Young

5

man, there is a great constructive job waiting for you and if you don't do it now you will only have to do it later under much more difficult circumstances.' So he rubbed a magic lamp of contributions . . . 'I know what's best for boys,' he said, and those Texas oilmen kicked in.

What I liked to do was get in my room against the radiator and play records and read the Little Blue Books put out by Haldeman-Julius, free-thinker and benevolent agnostic . . . Remy de Gourmont . . . Baudelaire . . . Guy de Maupassant . . . Anatole France . . . and I started writing allegories put in a vaguely Oriental setting, with dapper jewel thieves over the wine, engaged in philosophical discussions I prefer not to remember.

'To observe one's actions with detachment while making them as amusing as possible seem to me . . .'

'Very interesting,' said the imperturbable detective popping up from behind a potted rubber plant. 'You are all under arrest.'

I had a bad rep with the other boys . . . 'burns incense in his room . . . reading French books . . .' Later at Harvard during summer trips to Europe I started satirical novels about the people I met; one of them begins '"But you see I don't know much about love," she said coyly, twisting an old-fashioned.'

Then I had an English period, gentlemen adventurers and all that . . .

'My god, that poor old chief!' He broke down sobbing.

The other looked at him coldly and raised an eyebrow: 'Well after all, Reggie, you didn't expect him to *give us* the emeralds, did you?'

'I don't know what I expected, but not *that piranha* fish!'

'It was much the easiest and most convenient method.'

'I can't stick it, Humphreys, Give me my share, I'm clearing off.'

'Why certainly.' He took seven magnificent emeralds from the side pocket of his yellow silk suit and placed them on the table. With a quiet smile he pushed four stones to Reggie.

Reggie was touched. 'I mean, hang it all, it was your idea, Humphreys, and you did most of the work.'

'Yes Reggie, you funked it.'

'Then why?'

'I am thinking of Jane.'

Reggie made a hasty exit, 'I can't thank you enough' over his shoulder. Humphreys leaned forward, looking at the three emeralds quizzically.

'You'll be missing your mates, won't you now? . . . Ali!'

'Yes master.'

'A white man has just left. He is carrying four green stones. I want those stones, do you understand Ali?'

'Yes master I understand.' Exit Ali, fingering his kris.

And *then* I read Oscar Wilde. Dorian Gray and Lord Henry gave birth to Lord Cheshire, one of the most unsavory characters in fiction, a mawkishly sentimental Lord Henry . . . Seven English gentlemen there in the club, planning an expedition to the Pole:

'But *which* pole, Bradford?'

'Oh hang it all, who cares?'

'Why Reggie, you're as excited as a child!'

'I am, and I glory in it — let's forget we were ever gentlemen!'

'You seem to have done that already,' said Lord Cheshire acidly.

But it seems the cynical Lord Cheshire had more kindness in him than all the others put together when the supplies gave out . . . 'Poor Reggie there, rotten with scurvy, I can't bear to look at him, and Stanford is cracking, and there have been rumors about Cuthbert . . . Morgan drinks all day, and James is hitting the pipe . . .' So I leave him there on an ice floe, rotten with scurvy, giving his last lime juice to Reggie and lying bravely about it.

'Have you had yours?' said the boy softly.

'Yes,' said Lord Cheshire, 'I've had mine.'

And I wrote a story for *True Confessions*, about a decent young man who gets on the dope. He was grieving the loss of a favorite dog, sitting on a park bench looking at the lake, smell of burning leaves . . .

'Hello kid, mind if I sit down?' The man was thin and grey with pinpoint eyes, the prison shadow in them like something dead. 'If you don't mind my saying so, you look down in the dumps about something.'

In a burst of confidence the young man told him about the dog. '. . . he went back inside the burning house. You see, he thought I was in there.'

'Kid, I got a pinch of something here make you forget about that old dead dog . . .'

That's how it started. Then he fell into the hands of a sinister hypnotist who plied him with injections of marijuana.

'Kill, kill, kill.' The words turned relentlessly in his brain, and

7

he walked up to a young cop and said 'If you don't lock me up I shall kill you.' The cop sapped him without a word. But a wise old detective in the precinct takes a like to the boy, sets him straight and gets him off the snow. It was a hard fight but he made it. He now works in a hardware store in Ottawa, Illinois . . . the porch noise, home from work . . . 'And if any kind stranger ever offers me some pills that will drive all my blues away, I will simply call a policeman.'

A story about four jolly murderers was conceived in the Hotel La Fonda on a rare trip to Santa Fe when I was feeling guilty about masturbating twice in one day. A middle-aged couple, very brash and jolly; the man says 'Sure and I'd kill my own grandmother for just a little kale . . .'

'We have regular rates of course,' the woman observed tartly.

I formed a romantic attachment for one of the boys at Los Alamos and kept a diary of this affair that was to put me off writing for many years. Even now I blush to remember its contents. During the Easter vacation of my second year I persuaded my family to let me stay in St. Louis, so my things were packed and sent to me from the school and I used to turn cold thinking maybe the boys are reading it aloud to each other.

When the box finally arrived I pried it open and threw everything out until I found the diary and destroyed it forthwith, without a glance at the appalling pages. This still happens from time to time. I will write something I think is good at the time and looking at it later I say, my God, tear it into very small pieces and put it into somebody else's garbage can. I wonder how many writers have had similar experiences. An anthology of such writing would be interesting.

Fact is, I had gotten a real sickener — as Paul Lund, an English gangster I knew in Tangier, would put it . . . 'A young thief thinks he has a license to steal and then he gets a real sickener like five years maybe.'

This lasted longer. The act of writing had become embarrassing, disgusting, and above all *false*. It was not the sex in the diary that embarrassed me, it was the terrible falsity of the emotions expressed. I guess Lord Cheshire and Reggie were too much for me — for years after that, the sight of my words written on a page hit me like the sharp smell of carrion when you turn over a dead dog with a stick, and this continued until 1938. I had written myself an eight-year sentence.

Cambridge, Massachusetts, 1938 . . . I was doing graduate

work in anthropology at Harvard and at the same time Kells Elvins, an old school friend from John Burroughs, was doing graduate work in Psychology. We shared a small frame house on a quiet tree-lined street beyond the Commodore Hotel. He had many talks about writing and started a detective story in the Dashiell Hammett/Raymond Chandler line. This picture of a ship captain putting on women's clothes and rushing into the first lifeboat was suddenly *there* for both of us. We read all the material we could find in Widener's Library on the Titanic, and a book based on the Morro Castle disaster called *The Left-handed Passenger*.

On a screened porch we started work on a story called *Twilight's Last Gleamings* which was later used almost verbatim in *Nova Express*. I was trying to contact Kells to see if he had the original manuscript and to tell him that I was using the story under both our names when his mother wrote me that he had died in 1961.

I see now that the curse of the diary was broken temporarily by the act of collaboration. We acted out every scene and often got on laughing jags. I hadn't laughed like that since my first tea-high at eighteen when I rolled around the floor and pissed all over myself. I remember the rejection note from Esquire: 'Too screwy and not effectively so for us.'

I liked to feel that manuscript in my hands and read it over with slow shameless chuckles. The words seemed to come through us, not out of us. I have a recurrent writer's dream of picking up a book and starting to read. I can never bring back more than a few sentences; still, I know that one day the book itself will hover over the typewriter as I copy the words already written there.

After that I lost interest again and the years from 1938 to 1943 were almost entirely unproductive. In 1943 I met Kerouac and Ginsberg. Kerouac and I collaborated on a novel based on the Carr-Kammerer case, which we decided not to publish, and again I lost interest in writing.

I can remember only one attempt between 1943 and 1949. I was living in Algiers, Louisiana, across the river from New Orleans. I was on heroin at the time and went over to New Orleans every day to score. One day I woke up sick and went across the river, and when I got back I tried to recapture the painful over-sensitivity of junk sickness, the oil slick on the river, the hastily-parked car.

Next set is Mexico City 1948–1950 where I started writing *Junky*. Once again we had trouble with the middle-class Mexican neighbors, who suspected me to be a dope fiend, and and the children screamed at me in the street: *'Vicioso.'* We lived in a two-story house behind Sears Roebuck, off Insurgentes. I was attending Mexico City College on the G.I. Bill, studying Mayan and Aztec history and Mayan language. The Mexico City College boys hung out in a bar called the Bounty where I once shot a mouse with a .22 pistol. In Mexico I always carried some sort of gun.

This was during the reign of Presidente Aleman, and the *mordida* was king. A vast pyramid of bribes reached from the cop on the beat to the Presidente . . . 'Your paper very bad Meester.' And for every real cop there were two or three professional brothers of cops with huge badges in their pockets and .45s stuck down into the inside holsters as I have seen only in Mexico. These holsters clip on the belt with the holster part inside the pants and so were easier to conceal with the coat buttoned. Many times I have been woken up by some friend from Mexico City College at the door with two or more cops who have caught him with some weed or a gun. He is taking up a collection to buy them off.

On this set an unpublished novel called *Queer* was also written. I remember the editor of Ace Books who published *Junky* said he would go to jail if he ever published *Queer*. I have been looking through it. Charles-Henri Ford's and Parker Tyler's *The Young and Evil* is shocking by contrast. Thanks to Allen Ginsberg and Carl Solomon, *Junky* was published in 1953. I was in South America at the time and the account of this trip became *The Yage Letters*. These were typed out from handwritten notes in offices where you use a typewriter for so much per hour in Bogotà and Lima.

Late 1953 I spent in New York sharing an apartment with Allen Ginsberg. At this time I first met Gregory Corso. In January of 1954 I went to Tangier and settled in a male brothel at no. 1 Calle de los Arcos kept by the famous Tony Dutch. I was on junk and did very little writing at the time. There were, however, a few fragments that were later used in *Naked Lunch*. Understandably there was some neighbor trouble: 'You like beeg one Meester?' And Tony constantly moaned, 'My house is so watched at by the Arabics.'

In 1955 I moved to the Villa Muniria at the corner of Cook Street and Magellanes. It was owned by a Belgian at the time and Paul Lund, a gangster from Birmingham, was also staying there. I saw quite a lot of him and used some of his stories in *Naked Lunch*. Later that year I moved into a house in the Casbah owned by Jim Wylie where there was no neighbor trouble since I sat around all day shooting junk and once dripped blood all over Paul Bowles' first edition of *One Arm* by Tennessee Williams.

In 1956 I went to London and took the apomorphine cure with Doctor John Dent. *Naked Lunch* would never have been written without Doctor Dent's treatment. The cure completed, I spent the summer with Alan Ansen in Venice. It was during this summer that A.J.'s Annual Party took shape and the gondola scene was written. Some of the Border City material was also written at this time and the concept of Freelandt evolved. Here too I disgraced myself by getting drunk at Peggy Guggenheim's palazzo.

I left Venice in late August and went to Tripoli, arriving in time for the Suez Crisis and a general strike. The American Consulate wasn't at all helpful and still less so in Algiers, where I got stuck on my way back to Tangier with all planes booked solid for three weeks and had to wire home for money and left by train without the necessary permits against advice of the Consulate. I was in Algiers for about a week during the war and used to eat lunch in a milk bar that was later bombed. There are a number of references to this incident in later writings.

Back in Tangier in September of 1956, I settled in a room on the garden at the Villa Muniria. For the first time in my life I began writing full-time and the material from which *Naked Lunch* was later abstracted and a good deal of the material that went into *The Soft Machine* and *The Ticket that Exploded* was produced at this time. Often I would take a notebook to dinner with me and make notes while I ate. During this period I was making mahjoun every day.

Between 1956 and 1958 I saw a number of visitors in Tangier. Jack Kerouac was there in 1957, Allen Ginsberg and Peter Orlovsky in the same year. Alan Ansen made several trips to Tangier and helped me type the manuscript. In 1957 I made a trip to Scandinavia and wrote some of the Freelandt section for *Naked Lunch* in a cubicle room in Copenhagen.

In 1958 I moved to Paris and took up residence at no. 9, rue Git-le-coeur on the recommendation of Allen Ginsberg who was living there with Peter Orlovsky. I had a suitcase full of manuscripts with me, but Maurice Girodias of Olympia Press had rejected the first version of *Naked Lunch*. Other rejections from American publishers followed, and I was again losing interest in writing.

It was Allen Ginsberg who insisted that I send some short extracts to *The Chicago Review* which was then edited by Irving Rosenthal. The *Big Table* issue followed. One morning in room 15 at 9 rue Git-le-coeur I received a visit from Sinclair Beiles, whom I had known previously in Tangier. He was working for Girodias, who, after seeing the *Big Table* issue, now wanted to publish *Naked Lunch*. He wanted a complete manuscript in two weeks. With the help of Brion Gysin and Sinclair the manuscript was finished in two weeks and a month later the book was published.

In the summer of 1959 Brion Gysin showed me the use of cut-ups. *Minutes to Go* and *Exterminator!* followed. Brion Gysin also demonstrated the use of cut-ups on the tape recorder and my subsequent experiments with tape recorders, carried out in Paris, London, Tangier, New York, all date from that summer.

In the fall of 1959 I moved to London and stayed in the Empress Hotel at 25 Lillie Road, which was to be my headquarters for the next year and a half. By the spring and summer of 1961, I was back in Tangier in my old garden room at the Villa Muniria, and it was here that I first started making photo-montages. This happened after a bad trip on DMT, which is described in *The Night Before Thinking* . . . the sensation of being in a white-hot safe. The following day, a sudden cool grey mist came in from the sea and covered the waterfront and I spread some photos out on the bed with a grey silk dressing-gown from Gibraltar along with several other objects and I photographed the ensemble. During that summer I made many of these montages in different ways and combinations. Ian Sommerville arrived during the summer and took over the technical aspect of the montages. Also present were: Tim Leary, Allen Ginsberg, Alan Ansen, Paul Bowles, Michael Portman and Gregory Corso . . . the psychedelic summer.

In the fall of 1961 I spent a month in New York, where I started *Nova Express*. When I returned to England, my work with photo-montages and tape-recorders continued and in early 1962 I moved to an apartment sublet from Marion Boyars at 52 Lancaster Terrace in London, which I shared with Michael Portman. In a basement apartment I shared with Ian

Sommerville I prepared a show with his assistance. I also wrote some poems for David Bud's exhibition of sculpture in Paris.

In the summer of 1962, Ian and I went to Tangier where after some house-hunting we unwisely rented an Arab house at 4 calle Larachi. My son Billy arrived during the summer. *Esquire* took some photos of the house and of Billy and myself which were later used as an article.

We did not start to have real neighbor trouble until after the Kennedy assassination, but the trouble became acute after New Year's of 1964. I had just returned from a television appearance in London with Alex Trocchi in which we were interviewed by Dan Farsons. Arriving in England for this show, I was stopped and searched by Customs. I think the word had been passed along by some snotty Vice-Consul in the American Consulate in Tangier. When I got back, we were under continual harrassment from the neighbors and I had no money to move. I started keeping a diary and decorating files with photos; later I started keeping scrapbooks.

Early in May my first substantial payment came through from Grove Press and I moved into 16 rue Delacroix, the Loteria Building. The work with scrapbooks continued and Antony Balch arrived during the summer to shoot some of the scenes from *Cut-Ups*. In December, I returned to America by boat and arriving at Customs got the 'right-this-way' treatment. Two narcs and three Customs agents spent three solid hours pawing through my books and papers and photos, reading them and commenting.

I stayed in New York from 1964 until September 1965, at the Hotel Chelsea and in a loft at 210 Centre Street. There Brion and I assembled *The Third Mind*. Antony Balch came over from London to shoot more scenes for *Cut-Ups* and I did a lot of scrapbook work. Brion frequently remonstrated with me to leave these experiments and write some straight narrative.

Returning to England in September 1965, Brion and I were searched at the airport. After going through Customs and Immigration, an official walked out after us . . . and once again agents pawed through my papers. 'What do you cart these about for?' one said, holding up some Magic Markers/flash forward to being caught by a black subway guard, writing AH POOK IS HERE on the subway wall . . . 'You a grown man, writing on the wall!' New York City, April 30, 1972 . . .

We were limited to a stay in England of one month. Obviously, the American Narcotics Department had passed the word along. Lord Goodman, Michael Portman's solicitor and Chairman of the Arts Council, straightened out this passport difficulty. I settled in at the Hotel Rushmore at 11 Trebovir Road, Earl's Court. A number of tape-recorder experiments, described in *The Invisible Generation*, were carried out here with Ian Sommerville, who had a sound studio placed at his disposal by Paul McCartney.

By 1967, when I had moved into 8 Duke Street, Saint James's, I had such an overrun on tape-recorders, cameras and scrapbooks that I couldn't look at them, and started writing straight narrative and essays which later found their way into *The Wild Boys* and *The Job*. I made several trips to Tangier, to rework *The Ticket that Exploded*, and returned to Morocco and Marrakesh, where I started a first draft of *The Wild Boys*. In 1968, January through April, I was at Saint Hill in England, studying Scientology. In 1968, I covered the Democratic Convention in Chicago for *Esquire*.

My Own Business

Brion Gysin, Stewart Gordon, and I were sitting in front of a little Spanish café in Tangier when this middle-aged Spaniard walked by, and we all gasped: 'My God, that's a harmless-looking person!' I'd noticed him around town, and spotted him as a real M.O.B.ist: which is nothing special, just minds his own business of staying alive and thinks that what other people do is other people's business.

The old hop-smoking rod-riding underworld had a name for it: 'a member of the Johnson family.' Wouldn't rush to the law if he smelled hop in the hall, doesn't care what fags in the back room are doing, stands by his word. Good man to do business with. They are found in all walks of life. The cop who slipped me a joint in a New Orleans jail, for instance. Or when I was pushing junk in New York back in 1948, the hotel clerk who stopped me in the lobby: 'I don't know how to say this, but there is something wrong about the people who come to your room.' (Something wrong is putting it softly: ratty junkies with no socks, dressed in three boosted suits puffing out, carrying radios torn from the living car, trailing wires like entrails. 'This isn't a hock shop!' I scream. 'Get this shit out of here!' Regaining my composure I say severely, 'You are lowering the entire tone of my establishment.') 'So I just wanted to warn you to be careful and tell those people to watch what they say over the phone . . . if someone else had been at the switchboard . . .'

And a hotel clerk in Tunis; I handed him some money to put in the safe. He put the money away and looked at me: 'You do not need a receipt Monsieur.' I looked at him and saw that he was a Johnson, and knew that I didn't need a receipt.

Yes, this world would be a pretty easy and pleasant place to live in if everybody could just mind his own business and let others do the same. But a wise old black faggot said to me years ago: 'Some people are shits, darling.' I was never able to forget it.

Mexican druggist throwing a script back at me: 'We do not serve dope fiends.' It's like Mr. Anslinger said: 'The laws must express society's disapproval of the addict.'

Most of the trouble in this world has been caused by folks who can't mind their own business, because they have no business of their own to mind, any more than a smallpox virus has. Now your virus is an *obligate cellular parasite*, and my contention is that evil is quite literally a virus parasite occupying a certain brain area which we may term the RIGHT center. The mark of a basic shit is that he has to be *right*. And right here we must make a distinction between a hard-core virus-occupied shit and a plain, ordinary, mean no-good son of a bitch. Some of these sons of bitches don't cause any trouble at all, just want to be left alone and are only dangerous when molested, like the Brown Recluse. Others cause minor trouble, like barroom fights and bank robberies. To put it country simple, Anslinger was an obligate shit; Dillinger, Jesse James and Billy the Kid were just sons of bitches.

This *right* virus has been around for a long time, and perhaps its most devoted ally has been the Christian Church: from the Inquisition to the Conquistadores, from the American Indian Wars to Hiroshima, they are RIGHT RIGHT RIGHT. If the Christian Church has given the virus a nice long home, it has also sustained a number of evictions in the past forty years.

When I was in high school in the 1920's, anybody expressing doubts about our treatment of the Indians, capital punishment, the natural inferiority of blacks, the abomination of being a flit* or a dope fiend, would have been shunned by his schoolmates as a dangerous radical or practitioner of the hideous vices he defended.

Yes, quite a change, and quite a few points gained for the M.O.B.ists: virtual abolition of censorship, decriminalization of pot, gay rights, and segregation issues at least out in the open and a lot better than they were forty years ago, and a growing recognition, even in official quarters, that victimless crimes should be removed from the books or subject to minimal penalties. This trend towards sanity has brought the last-ditch dedicated shits out into the open, screaming with rage. Victimless crime, the assumption that what a citizen does in the privacy of his own dwelling is nonetheless someone else's business and therefore subject to denunciation and punishment, is the very lifeline of the *right* virus. Cutting off this air line would have the same action as interferon, which blocks the oxygen from certain virus strains.

* 'Flit' was a 1920 word for a queer. Since Flit was also an insecticide, such pleasantries as 'Quick Henry, Navarro!' made the rounds.

16

M.O.B. opponents cling to the victimless-crime concept, equating drug-taking or private sexual behaviour with robbery and murder. If the right to mind one's own business is recognized, the whole shit position is untenable, and Hell hath no more vociferous fury than an endangered parasite.

The Reverend Braswell, in the *Denver Post*: 'The United States shouldn't be forced to accept perverted sexual practices under the guise of human rights. I refuse to say we are dealing with human rights, we are dealing with sexual perversion. Speak out against these filthy dreamers. The Civil Rights Act is national suicide. The God of this Universe, He doesn't change. God's attitude to wrong is the same since Adam. The Bible classifies homosexuality along with murder, stealing, inventions of evil ruthlessness and God hatred. Homosexuality is an abomination to God and should never be recognized as a legal human right any more than robbery or murder.' And a letter to the Editor: 'We should reform the marijuana laws by making them tougher. President Carter's proposal to scrap Federal laws relating to marijuana is shocking.'

One is tempted to seek a total solution to the shit problem: Mass Assassination Day. M.A.D. Slaughter the shits of the world like cows with the aftosa. Then we'll all feel a lot better. 'It was like being cured of clap after twenty dripping years,' a survivor reported ... Perhaps we could accomplish the salubrious work with a virus designed to attack the already occupied RIGHT centers in the brain, inflaming and irritating these centers so that the target, muttering and finally screaming imprecations, dies in convulsions of rightness. It was known as Righteous Fever; old men need it special.

Here's an old fuck in his British club, writing a letter to *The Times* demanding the restoration of capital punishment and the whipping post and recruitment of all layabouts and 'hippies' into a labor battalion — suddenly he bares his teeth and shouts at the top of his voice: 'BLOODY HIPPIES!'

Shocked faces look up from newspapers as he falls to the carpet, kicking and spitting blood, his pants steaming with urine and excrement.

'Well now the Reverend he preaches up a pretty strong sermon and that's all right up to a point, but folks want to go home and eat lunch ... so when he gets on about the sinners in Hell, how their very bowels burst open in the fire throwing hot shit all over each other, "wallowing in their own boiling filth" as he put it, Old Man Brink got up and said "I think we've heard about enough of this, Reverend."'

'But the Reverend is bellowing out the *Battle Hymn of the Republic*:

'"He is trampling out the vintage where the grapes of wrath are stored —"

'He shits in his pants and spits blood ten feet, and everybody sees his pants is sticking out in front all indecent and the Sheriff says "He must be an abomination from the Bible to pull these scandals," so we burned the Church with the Reverend in it.'

Probably the most effective tactic is to alter the conditions on which the virus subsists. That is the way various manifestations of the RIGHT virus have disappeared in the past, as in the Inquisition. Conditions change, and that virus guise is ignored and forgotten. We have seen this happen many times in the past forty years. With the RIGHT virus offset, perhaps we can get the whole show out of the barnyard and into Space.

Les Voleurs

Writers work with words and voices just as painters work with colors; and where do these words and voices come from? Many sources: conversations heard and overheard, movies and radio broadcasts, newspapers, magazines, yes, and *other writers*; a phrase comes into the mind from an old western story in a pulp magazine read years ago, can't remember where or when: 'He looked at her, trying to read her mind — but her eyes were old, unbluffed, unreadable.' There's one that I lifted.

The County Clerk sequence in *Naked Lunch* derived from contact with the County Clerk in Cold Springs, Texas. It was in fact an elaboration of his monologue, which seemed merely boring at the time, since I didn't know yet that I was a writer. In any case, there wouldn't have been any County Clerk if I had been sitting on my ass waiting for my 'very own words'. You've all met the ad man who is going to get out of the rat race, shut himself up in a cabin, and write the Great American Novel. I always tell him, 'Don't cut your input, B.J. — you might need it.' So many times I have been stuck on a story line, can't see where it will go from here; then someone drops around and tells me about fruit-eating fish in Brazil. I got a whole chapter out of that. Or I buy a book to read on the plane, and there is the answer; and there's a nice phrase too, 'sweetly inhuman voices'. I had a dream about such voices before I read *The Big Jump* by Leigh Brackett, and found that phrase.

Look at the surrealist moustache on the Mona Lisa. Just a silly joke? Consider where this joke can lead. I had been working with Malcolm McNeil for five years on a book entitled *Ah Pook Is Here*, and we used the same idea: Hieronymus Bosch as the background for scenes and characters taken from the Mayan codices and transformed into modern counterparts. That face in the Mayan Dresden Codex will be the barmaid in this scene, and we can use the Vulture God over here. Bosch, Michaelangelo, Renoir, Monet, Picasso — steal anything in sight. You want a certain light on your scene? Lift it from Monet. You want a 1930's backdrop? Use Hopper.

The same applies to writing. Joseph Conrad did some superb

descriptive passage on jungles, water, weather; why not use them verbatim as background in a novel set in the tropics? Continuity by so-and-so, description and background footage from Conrad. And of course you can kidnap someone else's characters and put them in a different set. The whole gamut of painting, writing, music, film, is yours to use. Take Molly Bloom's soliloquy and give it to your heroine. It happens all the time anyway; how many times have we had Romeo and Juliet served up to us, and Calille grossed forty million in *The Young Lovers*. So let's come out in the open with it and steal freely.

My first application of this principle was in *Naked Lunch*. The interview between Carl Peterson and Doctor Benway is modelled on the interview between Razumov and Councillor Mikulin in Conrad's *Under Western Eyes*. To be sure, there is no resemblance between Benway and Mikulin, but the form of the interview, Mikulin's trick of unfinished sentences, his elliptical approach, and the conclusion of the interview are quite definitely and consciously used. I did not at the time see the full implications.

Brion Gysin carried the process further in an unpublished scene from his novel *The Process*. He took a section of dialogue *verbatim* from a science fiction novel and used it in a similar scene. (The science fiction novel, appropriately, concerned a mad scientist who devised a black hole into which he disappeared.) I was, I confess, slightly shocked by such overt and *traceable* plagiarism. I had not quite abandoned the fetish of originality, though of course the whole sublime concept of total theft is implicit in cut-ups and montage.

You see, I had been conditioned to the idea of words as *property* — one's 'very own words' — and consequently to a deep repugnance for the black sin of plagiarism. Originality was the great virtue. I recall a boy who was caught out copying an essay from a magazine article, and this horrible case discussed in whispers . . . for the first time the dark word 'plagiarism' impinged on my consciousness. Why, in a Jack London story a writer shoots himself when he finds out that he has, without knowing it, plagiarized another writer's work. He did not have the courage to be a writer. Fortunately, I was made of sterner or at least more adjustable stuff.

Brion pointed out to me that I had been stealing for years: 'Where did that come from — "Eyes old, unbluffed, unreadable?" And that — "inflexible authority?" And that — "arty type, no principles." And that — and that — and that?' He looked at me sternly.

'*Vous etes un voleur honteux* . . . a closet thief.' So we drew up a manifesto . . .

Les Voleurs

Out of the closet and into the museums, libraries, architectural monuments, concert halls, bookstores, recording studios and film studios of the world. Everything belongs to the inspired and dedicated thief. All the artists of history, from cave painters to Picasso, all the poets and writers, the musicians and architects, offer their wares, importuning him like street vendors. They supplicate him from the bored minds of school children, from the prisons of uncritical veneration, from dead museums and dusty archives. Sculptors stretch forth their limestone arms to receive the life-giving transfusion of flesh as their severed limbs are grafted onto Mister America. *Mais le voleur n'est pas pressé* — the thief is in no hurry. He must assure himself of the quality of the merchandise and its suitability for his purpose before he conveys the supreme honor and benediction of his theft.

Words, colors, light, sounds, stone, wood, bronze belong to the living artist. They belong to anyone who can use them. Loot the Louvre! *A bas l'originalité*, the sterile and assertive ego that imprisons as it creates. *Vive le vol* — pure, shameless, total. We are not responsible. Steal anything in sight.

Beauty and the Bestseller

If your purpose is to make a lot of money on a book or a film, there are certain rules to observe. You're aiming for the general public, and there are all sorts of things the general public just doesn't want to see or hear. A good rule is never expect a general public to experience anything they don't want to experience. You don't want to scare them to death, knock them out of their seats, and above all you don't want to puzzle them.

There are certain bestseller formulas. For example, something that the movie-going or reading public knows something about and about which they want to know more: the Mafia, how a hotel is run, what happens in General Motors, in TV, advertising, and in Hollywood.

Now, if they don't know anything about a subject, no matter how good it looks it won't look good to them. I had learned this years ago raising winter vegetables in the Rio Grande Valley in Texas. There are three main areas for winter vegetables: California, Florida, and the Rio Grande Valley. If the tomatoes freeze in one area or better still, in two areas, it boosts the price of tomatoes in another area. There was this one farmer who had practically the only parsnips on the winter vegetable market, and he thought he had a fortune. But it turned out they were so rare that the ordinary housewife didn't want to buy them. She had forgotten what a parsnip looked like and didn't want to contact any such unknown winter vegetable. So there's such a thing as being too rare.

The other formula is the menace, the challenge posed by the menace and the final resolution when the menace is fully dissipated.

The menace can be an epidemic, an enemy about to spray nerve gas on New York City or poison the water supply, or even a revived prehistoric monster. But here you have to be very careful; the general public won't want to be really frightened or shaken up too much, just a little bit. The horror film formula involves a measure of extortion: you're paying *not* to see something that's *really* horrible, you are paying to see Willard's nice rats and *not to see* rats eating the genitals off a screaming infant.

So we combine these two formulas for a sure-fire hit . . .

The set is a biological warfare center. What goes on behind these walls? See what I mean? We are taking the reader right past the MP's at the gate, into Top Secret Classified areas. Bitter staff rivalries and intrigues — the lady virologist who loves Doktor Hester, who has eyes for the FBI lady who pretends to be a receptionist . . . Here is a staff meeting where Professor Steinplatz denounces as nonsense Doktor Hester's Anthrax 38: 'It is time we got so out from the barnyard.' Doktor Hester has other projects; he bides his time.

Now here's the beginning: Louie the Light opens his beady black eyes and looks cautiously around the room. He stands up groggily and looks at a door in front of him. He shivers, remembering an occasion when with his sex centers inflamed by electrodes he had started through that door towards a stunning albino with pink eyes. Just as he touched the door an agonizing shock twisted his lean body as a blinding light shone straight into his pleasure-dilated pupils. After that he couldn't see for five days during which he was given no food. It was Doktor Hester who named him Louie the Light from the number of lights to which he had been exposed.

Footsteps. Key in the lock. Louie conceals himself behind a centrifuge. Voices . . . 'So now Doktor we will see your so interesting Wilhelm Hester Virus 23, nein?' No one notices a grey shadow as it streaks down the hall.

Louie the Light can hardly walk by the time he reaches Highway 97. LIGHTS! He squeaks with terror. The next second a tire flattens him into a bloody blob, his fear-dilated eyes, long yellow teeth and curled tail looking up at the mud guard. Louie has seen the light. Ten minutes later, the driver (subsequently identified at St. Vincent's Hospital as Walter Winch, travelling X-ray equipment salesman) is in a gas line at Broadway and 23rd Street.

Meanwhile, in Doktor Hester's laboratory, Professor Steinplatz points dramatically to an empty cage. 'Where is this wondrous rat? This Louie the Lighted?'

Doktor Hester turns pale. He realizes with appalling clarity that he has made one of the great goofs of history, besides which Verdun, the invasion of Russia by Napoleon and Hitler, the Dardanelles, are but grains of sand on a vast radioactive empty beach. Within days Virus B-23 rages through the cities of the world like a topping forest fire.

Newscaster: 'Virus B-23 is one of the most contagious diseases ever to appear on this planet and it shows such an ability to mutate that a physician can never be sure he is dealing with a case of B-23 until the hideous terminal symptoms supervene: an accelerated putrefaction accompanied by sexual frenzies, the victim rotting and performing obscene acts before the horrified eyes of his friends and family. In the end the victim disintegrates, giving off sepia puffs of noxious yellow vapours and deadly spores that infect anyone in the vicinity — and the people running from centers of infection spread the plague in concentric circles.'

At this point we start selling the movie rights. It can be a twenty-million dollar spectacular or it can be a low-budget winner shot right in the germ center . . . 'I feel terrible about the whole thing,' says Doktor Hester on TV. So finally the virus is brought under control, leaving bizarre mutations in its wake, some quite favorable — so that Doktor Hester becomes a hero of the virus. He gets together with the lady virologist and they realize there is something, well, *wrong* about what they have been doing. 'I guess we were just caught up in the rat race like everyone else and lost our moral compasses.' Their fingers creep together . . . 'Bill and I, well, we're going to devote the rest of our lives to ecology.' A naked mutant streaks by at fifty miles an hour taking twenty feet in a stride.

'Nice hopeful ending. What's wrong with it, K.E.?'

'Just about everything is wrong with it, B.J. You think nice Book-of-the-Month-Club ladies on the East Coast want to read about people like their own neighbors falling apart at a cocktail party and exposing themselves right in front of the Bensons, the Bradfields and the Johnsons? Is that your idea of mass appeal?'

'Well the kids will dig it. We could angle in some poignant love stories — you know the scene in the hospital where she is dying of B-23 . . . it's more dramatic than leukemia you see . . .'

'Such a thing as getting too dramatic B.J.'

'Well of course we don't bring on these scenes of terminal B-23 until the last reel. That builds up suspense and everybody wants to see the terminal stages just like they want to see the monster in a horror flick. So we bring on the monster which of course has given us the mutants and we end on a quiet nostalgic note . . . empty cities, nice gardens, very few people. Plenty of time, plenty of room, and plenty of everything for everybody. It's what everybody wants. Doktor Hester and the lady virologist decided it was all worth it for the fertilizer alone, for the corpses have laid down a vast, compost heap from which corn, wheat, potatoes, beans, peppers and broccoli will spring

24

in lush profusion. Back to the Garden of Eden . . . what's wrong with that?'

'Folks aren't going to like the way you got there B.J. You think the reader wants to be fertilizer to feed a bunch of freaks? They won't buy it B.J. I tell you, they just won't buy it. "So it should grow from my coffin?" snaps the Director when we show him the script. Can't we have a decent epidemic? Why, we could end up with an X rating. Putrefaction is enough already and will cost us heavy in special effects . . .'

'Well think about *The Devils* . . . sexual possession among the nuns . . . and the *Exorcist* . . . it's breaking all records.'

'Look, a few nuns five hundred years ago is one thing — one little girl is one thing. Two hundred million rotting citizens is another. The Book-of-the-Month-Club ladies don't want a thing like this dumped right in their laps . . . the reader likes a menace to keep its distance. The reading public and the movie-going public know little or nothing about biological weapons. And they don't want to know any more. Scrap the whole idea, it's terrible.'

'All right all right . . . so then how's this for an angle B.J.? The sex life of Siamese twins . . .'

So this business of writing bestsellers is not as easy as it seems. Even after you get through all the operators, all the manipulation and intrigue, you still have to be very sure that you've really got something that you can sell.

Additional remarks on *The Godfather*: The writer knows his subject and his characters; the book took seven years to write. These are real-life characters with real-life counterparts. The singer is Frank Sinatra (Tony Bennett?). The Godfather is Carlo Gambino. The doctor . . . the lovable drunk who has been written up in an article about Hollywood lushes. Not only is the reader getting inside information, he is getting real people and events. This is fact, fictionalized and presented in a palatable form with suspense and climaxes. You have to know the subject and the people to write it, and there's a lot of hard work involved.

Frederick Forsyth conforms even more closely to the formula of fictionalized fact. He was a foreign correspondent, and he knows the subjects and the people he writes about. Information is carefully researched, the characters based on real-life counterparts he has interviewed and known. I recommend his books to anyone interested in writing fiction, whether he is trying to write a bestseller or not. The books are worth reading not just for the inside information on the subject of the book, but also for information on writing commercially, and organizing material. *The Day of the Jackal* is inside information on the attempts to assassinate de Gaulle. The whole subject of assassination is stated in the most basic terms. Remember, de Gaulle had real pros gunning for him: ex-army officers with money and weapons they knew how to use, an underground army in fact. So the Jackal, a real pro who sets out to assassinate de Gaulle on contract, is also up against real pros. You couldn't have gotten a real pro out of an American President.

De Gaulle, like all politicians, becomes his public newspaper image, and so his character is already in the area of journalism. You don't need first-class writing for a stock character. The Jackal is a bit better than good: anonymous handsome golf-pro eyes that cloud over just before he kills someone. No one can read his thoughts, not even the writer. In the end we are in doubt as to his existence.

The suspense formula is like symbolic logic. So many days to count down. The Day when he has to hit the General. What he does every day. What the whole combined police, secret service and army does to find him and terminate. Balance moves.

Non-fiction is easier and more profitable.

Of course writing like *Alive* is even more trouble than well researched fiction like *The Day of the Jackal*. The writer has to get down to Uruguay and get the ghouls to talk to him to scoop the whole tasty good thing before someone else does.

There is a type of bestseller that requires no research at all if you have the stomach for it. The self-help book will transform your whole life. *Your Erroneous Zones, Think and Grow Rich, Win Through Intimidation.* You just sit down and write it if you're the kind of person who can write something like that. *Your Erroneous Zones.* I really take off my hat to that title. It hits the reader right where he lives. And gooses him right up to the cash register. Well, those are no research books. Just windy old platitudes. There's one born every minute to buy it. He knows he doesn't know anything so he makes the wishful assumption that someone else does who is now going to share it with him and 8,000,000 others. Get the title first then write the book.

There is also a class of minimal research. Six books out now on the Bermuda Triangle using the same sources. Secret Life of Plants and Secrets of Plants. A hot subject is prolonging life. Other books out of course. But a snappy title like Rubber Youth . . . How to put out bum youth checks . . . Reviewing all the angles on novocaine in Rumania, monkey glands in Mexico in the 30's, aging theories, a month's research, a good pushy agent, a few good breaks and you have a Number 1.

Fiction can be written up to the level of the writer's ability. I don't mean they aren't carefully planned. I mean the writer is not pulling punches and writing down to the public. Bely knew a lot about sharks. It was his hobby so he sits down and writes it straight. Like I say, up to the level of the writer's ability. You don't sit down and concoct a bestseller. I've tried. Either the story runs away with you and gets out of hand and you write what you have to write, or else you strike lucky and get a subject the public wants anyway.

A Word to the Wise Guy

After teaching a class in Creative Writing a few years back, my own creative powers fell to an all-time low. I really had a case of writer's block, and my idealistic young assistant complained that I simply sat around the loft doing absolutely nothing — which was true. This gave me to think (as the French say): *Can* creative writing be taught? And am I being punished by the Muses for impiety and gross indiscretion in revealing the secrets to a totally unreceptive audience — like you start giving away hundred-dollar bills and nobody wants them . . . I also discovered that the image of 'William Burroughs' in my students' minds had little relation to the facts. They were disappointed because I wore a coat and tie to class; they had expected me to appear stark naked with a strap-on, I presume. In all, a disheartening experience.

'Creative Writing' — what does that mean? I would have liked to put them all off the career of writing. Be a plumber instead — (I felt like screaming) — and have your fucking king-size fridge full of Vienna sausages, chilled aquavit and Malvern spring water, and look at your color TV with remote-control switch and cuddle a .30-.30 on your lap, waiting for the deer season when all sensible citizens will be in their cellars with sandbags stacked around them. Or be a doctor for chrissakes — once you make the big-time as the best ass-hole doctor what can be got, you don't have to worry like next year there won't be no ass-holes to operate on. But next year maybe no ass-holes will buy my books . . .

All right, maybe two, three people in the class can't be dissuaded. My advice is get a good agent and a good tax accountant if you ever make any money, and remember, you can't eat fame. And you can't write unless you *want* to write, and you can't want to unless you feel like it. Say you're a doctor with a nice practice. You don't feel so well today — family troubles and other things you can't quite put a name to — and you just feel fucking terrible, as you slip a chlorophyll tablet in your mouth to cover three quick drinks — (that old bitch would

spread it all over Palm Beach, 'My *dear* he was *drunk . . .*')
Well you can still carry on and what the hell, quarter-grain of
morphine for each patient; no matter what is wrong with them,
they will feel better immediately and prize me as the best of
croakers. And if I get any sass from the Narcs, I'll just tell 'em,
'Well I'm off to work in the Bahrein Islands so you take over my
practice and shove it up your ass.' I mean, even if you don't feel
like practicing medicine, you can still do it. Same way with law;
you don't feel like trying a case, all you gotta do is get a
continuance and lay up smoking weed in Martha's Vineyard for
a month.

In these other professions you can always cover for not
feeling like doing it, but writing you didn't feel like doing ain't
worth shit. The profession has many advantages; sure, you can
ride out on a white shark to a villa in the Bahamas, or you can
spend twenty years teaching English in the Berlitz School,
writing the Great Book that nobody can read. James Joyce
wrote some of the greatest prose in the language — *The Dead*,
Dubliners — but could he stop there and write exquisite stories
about unhappy Irish Catholics from then on out? If so, they
would have rewarded him with the Nobel Prize. Now nobody
ever tells a doctor, 'Lissen Doc, your ass operations is the
greatest, many grateful queens is getting fucked again, but you
gotta do something *new* —' Of course he doesn't have to; it's the
same old ass. But a writer has to do something new, or he has to
standardize a product — one or the other. Like I could
standardize the queer Peter-Pan wild-boy product, and put it
out year after year like the Tarzan series; or I could write a
Finnegans Wake. So, I get this idea about a private eye and the
Cities of the Red Night . . . *Quien sabe*?

Or take the entertainment business; today you may be the
Top of the Pops, the rage of the café society . . . like Dwight
Fisk, who did those horrible double-entendre numbers back in
the Thirties — 'That's the man who pinched me in the Astor,
just below the mezzanine, and for several days your mother
wasn't seen; so now my little heart you know where you got
your start, from a pinch just below the mezzanine' — who in the
fuck wants to hear that noise anymore? But you won't see
any doctor, lawyer, engineer, architect who's got to be world
champion at his profession or else stand on a corner selling ties
with his brains knocked out. No atomic physicist has to worry,
people will always want to kill other people on a mass scale.
Sure, he's got the fridge full of sausages and spring water, just

like the plumber. Nothing can happen to him; grants, scholarships, a rainbow to his grave and a tombstone that glows in the dark.

Artists do however have a degree of freedom. A writer has little power, but he does have freedom, at least in the West, Mr. Yevtushenko. Think very carefully about this. Do you want to be merely the spokesman for accomplished power movers? The more power, the less freedom. A politician has almost no freedom at all. I am frequently asked, 'What would you do if you were President? What would you do if you were the dictator of America? What would you do if you had a billion dollars?' In the words of my friend Ahmed Jacoubi, 'This question is not personal opinion.' A prior question must be asked: 'How did you *get to be* the President, a dictator, a billionaire?' The answers to these questions will condition what you will do. For one is not magically teleported into these positions; one gets there by a series of discrete steps, each step hedged with conditions and prices.

To take a microcosmic example: my humble ambition to be Commissioner of Sewers for St. Louis, and my boyish dread of what I would do when I occupied this position. These dreams were outlined in an essay I wrote for *Harper's* in response to the question, 'When did you stop wanting to be President?' I imagined a soft sinecure, crooked sewer-piping deals, my house full of languid vicious young men described in the press as 'no more than lackeys to his majesty the Sultan of Sewers.' I supposed my position would be secured by the dirt I had on the Governor, and that I'd spend my afternoons in wild orgies or sitting around smoking the Sheriff's reefer and luxuriating in the stink from ruptured sewage lines for miles around.

But why should I have been appointed Commissioner of Sewers in the first place ? The duties are nominal; no skill is required. I am not appointed on my knowledge of sewers or my ability to do the job. Why, then? Well, perhaps I have worked for the Party for a number of years; I am due for a payoff. However, I must also have something to give in return. Perhaps I can sway some votes, which action on my part is contingent on my receiving some payoff? Or perhaps they expect me to take the rap for the piping deal. If so I will have to watch my step and the use of my signature. Perhaps they expect a contribution to the campaign fund, which I am in a position to swing, having access to people of wealth. One thing is sure — they expect something from me in return.

How an under-the-counter deal in cheap piping involves contractors, auditors, and a whole battery of fixes, fixers, and cover-ups, all of which have to be paid in favors and cash. So my house is *not* full of languid vicious young men — it is full of cigar-smoking bourbon-swilling fat-assed politicians and fixers. I have something on the Governor? I'd better be very damn careful he doesn't have something on *me*. The Commissioner, like Caesar's wife, must be above suspicion; certainly above the suspicion of sex orgies and drug use. I would have been out of my mind to compromise myself with the Sheriff. Sure, I can call on him to fix a parking ticket, but I'd better keep my hands off his confiscated marijuana unless others in higher positions are also involved. And even if I could wangle a few special police to guard the sewers against communistic sabotage, they would not be handsome youths. More likely I would be stuck with the Sheriff's retarded brother-in-law who can't make the grade as a night watchman, and with two or three other wash-outs from police and guard positions.

So if I can't do what I want as Commissioner of Sewers, still less can I do what I want as President of the United States. I will disband the Army and the Navy and channel the entire Defense budget into setting up sexual adjustment centers, will I? I'll legalize marijuana? Annul the Oriental Exclusion Act? Abolish income tax for artists and put the burden of taxation onto the very rich? I should live so long.

I think that Richard Nixon will go down in history as a true folk hero, who struck a vital blow to the whole diseased concept of the revered image and gave the American virtue of ir-reverence and skepticism back to the people.

Technology of Writing

When Anthony Burgess was teaching his course in creative writing, a student asked him: 'Why should you be up there teaching writing and not me?' A good question; and I wish I could give as definite an answer as can be given in regard to other subjects where the technology is more clearly defined. No one, unless he is himself an experienced pilot, asks why the pilot of an airliner should be in the cockpit and not him. The answer is that he knows how to fly the plane and you don't. Nor would a student of quantum mechanics, engineering, or mathematics ask such a question; the teacher is there because he knows more about the subject than the student. To say he knows more presupposes that there is something definite to know, that a technology exists and can be taught to qualified students.

How many writers have taken courses in creative writing? Some of them certainly. James Jones for one, who took a course with some literary lady who had her students imitate the styles of well-known writers ... write Hemingway for a month, Graham Greene for a month, and so forth. A good exercise I think. But there are certainly, I think, more writers who have not taken courses in writing than writers who have. How many pilots have taken courses in flying? All of them, we hope. How many physicists have taken courses in physics? All of them. Which brings us to the question I intend to raise in this course and to hopefully arrive at some answers. Is there a technology of writing? Can writing be taught?

As soon as we ask the question we realize that there is no simple yes-or-no answer, since there are many technologies of writing and a technique that is useful for one writer may be of no use to another. There is no way to write. So we will begin looking for *answers*, not *the* answer. A pilot must possess certain qualifications before he starts flying lessons. A degree of coordination, steady nerves, a certain level of intelligence. A student of physics must have a considerable aptitude for mathematics. The qualifications for a writer are not so definable. The ability to sit at a typewriter for many hours without distraction is certainly useful. The ability to endure solitude is useful but not essential. An ability to empathize with others, to see and hear what is in their minds, is useful — but some very great writers like Beckett have only one character and need no others.

In general, the more observant a writer is, the more he will find to write about. I recommend an exercise I have practiced for years: when walking down any street, try to *see* everyone on the street before he sees you. You will find that if you see others first they will *not* see you, and that gives you time to observe, or file for future use. I learned this exercise from an old Mafia don in Columbus, Ohio. If a writer is seen first he won't necessarily get shot, but he may miss a set or a character. Someone glimpsed in passing may be used as a character years later; some doorway or shop front may serve as a set. An absent-minded writer closes the doors of perception.

Genet said of a French writer who shall here be nameless: He does not have the courage to be a writer. What courage does he refer to? The courage of the inner exploration, the cosmonaut of inner space. The writer cannot pull back from what he finds because it shocks or upsets him, or because he fears the disapproval of the reader. Allied to this courage are persistence and the ability to endure discouragement. Any writer must do a great deal of bad writing and he may not know how bad it is at the time. Writers are not always good critics of their own work. Sinclair Lewis said, 'If you have just written something that you think is absolutely great and you can't wait to show it to someone, tear it up, it's terrible.' I have certainly had the experience of writing something I thought was the greatest, and reading it over a few days later said, 'My God tear it into very small pieces and put it in someone else's garbage can.' On the other hand, something that I did not think much of at the time may stand up very well on rereading. What I wish to point out is that the writer must be able to survive an uneven performance that would be disastrous in another profession. An actor or a musician must put on a certain level of performance, whereas a writer has time to edit and choose what he will eventually put out as the finished product.

I have never known a writer who was not at one time an avid reader. I believe it was T.S. Eliot who said that if a writer has a pretentious literary style, it is generally because he has not read enough books. Some knowledge of what *has* been done in writing is, I think, essential — just as a doctor or a lawyer must

33

be conversant with the literature in his field. A full-time professional writer does not as a rule get much time to read, so it is well to get your reading in early.

To recapitulate qualifications which are useful but not essential: the ability to endure the physical discipline of writing, that is, to sit at a typewriter and write; the ability to persist and to absorb the discouragement of rejection and the even deadlier discouragement that comes from your own bad writing; insight into the motives of others; ability to think in concrete visual terms; a grounding in general reading. Now assume that the student has at least some of these qualifications. What can he be taught about writing?

It is of course easier to tell someone how not to write than how to write. Remember for example that a bad title can sink a good book or a good one sell a bad book. But it can sink a film faster and deeper, because a film has just one shot to make it. A book with a bad title or a slow beginning may make a come-back — a film just gets one chance. Here again there are no absolute rules; but there are guidelines. A good title gives the reader an *image* and arouses his interest in the image. Bad titles convey negative images, refer to images which the audience cannot understand until they see the film, or convey no image at all. Titles of more than three words are to be avoided — such turn-off titles as 'The Marriage of a Young Stock Broker'. 'The Conformist' is a turn-off title. Those of you who have seen the film will know it is about a fascist who ends up denouncing his blind friend as a fascist when Mussolini falls. 'The Survival Artist' would have been a better title.

There is a definite technology for the negative use of words to cause confusion, to create and aggravate conflicts, and to discredit opponents. This is the opposite of what a writer does. Here, the more abstract words and meaningless statements there are, the better. This technology has been developed in the mass media by Hearst and others, refined in LIFE and TIME, and carried still further by the CIA in some subsidized literary periodicals. The technology for writing a turn-off review is so definite that one sentence will tell you when it is being used — and it is much more complicated than just saying derogatory things about the book. It is very important for any writer to be able to absorb unfair criticism calmly and, when given the opportunity, to reply to it. It is also good practice to write book reviews.

To return to the matter of technology, let us consider first the question of our materials: Words. Korzybski's book, *Science and Sanity*, is a great timesaver. The fact that a word is *not* the object it represents — that this desk, whatever it may be, is not the label 'desk' — fully realized, will save the student a lot of pointless verbal arguments. Look at abstract words that have no definite referent — words like communism, materialism, civilization, fascism, reductivism, mysticism. There are as many definitions as there are users of these words. According to Korzybski, a word that has no referent is a word that should be dropped from the language, and I would say, certainly from the vocabulary of the writer. For example, take the word 'fascism': what does it mean? What is the referent? Consider the phenomenon of Nazi Germany — the military expansion of an industrialized country; now consider South Africa — oppression designed to maintain a status quo; are these both fascism?

In short, we have so many different phenomena lumped under this word that the use of the word can only lead to confusion. So we can drop the word altogether and simply describe the various and quite different political phenomena. I have been accused of being an arch materialist and a bourgeois mystic. What do these words mean? Virtually nothing. And because they mean nothing you can argue about them for all eternity. Any words that have referents cannot be argued about; there it is — call it a desk, a table, call it whatever you like, but no argument is possible. All arguments stem from confusion, and all arguments are a waste of time unless your purpose is to cause confusion and waste time.

I have learned as lot about writing by writing film scripts. As soon as a writer starts writing a film script — that is, writing in terms of what appears on screen — he is no longer omniscient. He cannot for example inform the reader that 'It was a clear bright day in May of 1923 in St. Louis, Missouri.' How does the film audience know that the month is May, the year 1923, the locale St. Louis? This information must be shown on the screen, unless the writer falls back on the dubious expedient of the offstage voice. Or: 'As he left his house and turned onto Euclid Avenue that morning, he felt a chill of foreboding.' Did he indeed — and how is this to be shown on screen? Some incident must be presented that gave him this chill; perhaps someone passing him on the street who mutters something that may or may not be directed towards him — or he intercepts a malignant expression as someone passes on a bicycle. And such phrases as 'words cannot convey', 'indescribable', unspeakable', cannot be shown on screen. You cannot get away with an indescribable monster. The audience want to *see* the monster. That's what they are paying for. The ability to think in concrete visual terms is almost essential to a writer. Generally speaking, if he can't see it, hear it, feel it, smell it, he can't write it.

The impact of the mass media is more directly felt in films than in books. In the 1920's, gang war was box office year after year, but remember that there were no television pictures of gang war on screen. There were only still pictures and newspaper accounts. It was front-page news and people were interested because it was something going on which they could not see directly. Had they seen it day after day, like the terrorist activity in Belfast today, they would have lost interest. Image loses impact with use. Anyone like to try making a film about the IRA in Belfast? Or writing a book on the subject for that matter? People are fed up with the IRA in Belfast. Or how about the Arab terrorists? Call it 'Death in Munich?' World War II — there were of course films on location, but not all that many, and no TV cameras at the front. There have been a lot of successful films made since then, and at least two books: *From Here To Eternity* and *The Naked and the Dead*. But who has written a bestseller about the Vietnam War?

Dreams are a fertile source of material for writing. Years ago I read a book by John Dunne called *An Experiment with Time*. (1924). Dunne was an English physicist, and he observed that his dreams referred not only to past but also to future events. However, the future material, since it often seems trivial and irrelevant, will not be remembered unless it is written down. This got me into the habit of writing dreams down, and I have done this for about thirty years. I began writing dreams down long before I started to write. I have, over a period of years, turned up a number of future references; but much more important is the number of characters and sets I have obtained directly from dreams, and at least forty percent of my material derives from dreams. When I contact a character, I start building up an identikit picture. For example, I meet a character in a dream; then I may find a photo in a magazine that looks like the character, or I may meet someone who looks like him in some respect. Usually my characters are composites of many people — from dreams, photos, people I know and quite frequently characters in other writing. Over a period of years I have filled a number of scrapbooks with these identikit pictures.

Finally, I will examine the connections between so-called occult phenomena and the creative process. Are not all writers, consciously or not, operating in these areas?

One more thing: Sinclair Lewis said: 'If you want to be a writer, learn to type.' This advice is scarcely necessary now. So then sit down at your typewriter and write.

Creative Reading

Having given courses in creative writing, I have come to doubt whether writing can be taught. It is like trying to teach someone how to dream. So I now teach creative reading. A few comments or quotations can turn a receptive student onto a book, and learning to read with discrimination is a crucial step towards learning to write. Creative reading demands the active participation of the reader, and the first step is critical evaluation.

Matthew Arnold formulated three questions for a book critic to ask and answer:

1. What is the writer trying to do?
2. How well does he succeed in doing it?
3. Is it worth doing? Does the book achieve what he calls 'high seriousness'?

So what is the writer trying to do? Many critics disparage a writer because they don't like what he is trying to do, or because he is not trying to do something else.

Ask the second question and you are well on the way to creative reading and the useful exercise of putting what the book is about into one or two sentences. Take *Jaws*: Menace posed by great white shark eating the bathers and endangering the tourist trade.

Menace poses challenge. Man meets challenge. Menace is removed by protagonist. What is *The Great Gatsby* about? Poor boy loves rich girl. He loses rich girl to rich man and meets a violent death trying to turn back the clock and realise 'the last and greatest of human dreams.' What is *Lord Jim* about? Honor lost. Honor regained.

Now the third question poses itself. Is it worth doing? Art makes us aware of what we know and don't know that we know. Our conscious awareness, our ego, has been compared to the tip of the iceberg that appears above water. Fitzgerald shows us more of the iceberg, more of the hidden depths than O'Hara. He is literally a deeper writer. Gatsby touches us in a way that the protagonist of O'Hara's *Appointment in Samarra* does not.

Some other questions the creative reader can ask are: Does the writer have an ear for dialogue? Many good writers don't. Fitzgerald's characters are delineated more by his descriptive prose than by what they say. His dialogue tends to be wooden, with occasional flashes of brilliant insight as when Gatsby says about Daisy's voice: 'It's full of money.' John O'Hara, a much lesser writer, had a superb ear for dialogue.

Does the writer have a distinctive style? Style, the manner of writing, the choice of one word rather than another, may be so distinctive that you read one sentence and you know who wrote it: 'The hole in his forehead where the bullet went in was about the size of a pencil. The hole in the back of his head where the bullet came out was big enough to put your fist in if it was a small fist and you wanted to put it there.' Who else but Papa Hemingway could have penned these lines and challenged Dryden's hitherto undisputed title to the most atrocious conceit in the English language for his stunning lines on Lord Hasting's smallpox:

> 'Each little pimple had a tear in it
> To wail the fault its rising did commit.'

'In his youth he had considered raising alligators in Florida. But there was no security in the alligators.' Janey Bowles — who else?

'I had not ridden since I was ten years old when my horrible little black pony had at last been given away. How I hated it! Once it had broken out of the stable and had galloped through the roses and over the lawns, showing its awful yellow teeth,' Denton Welch, *Maiden Voyage*.

Style can become a limitation and a burden. Hemingway was a prisoner of his style. No one can talk like the characters in Hemingway except the characters in Hemingway. His style in the wildest sense finally killed him. 'I'd shoot down my own mother,' he wrote in a letter to a friend 'if she was a mallard and I could lead her sweet and clean with no. 4 load.'

Papa is explaining to Papa about Hollywood. 'One can with honor sell one's soul in Hollywood. Everyone does it here,' he says. His style was hermetic. No escape for Papa. Mektoub. It was written. Sold his soul for a Safari. For a valorous wildebeest steak after a muscular martini. For the sheer joy of killing a charging rhino. 'Aye,' says the wise old hunter puffing on his pipe which he lights from a firebrand, 'That's a natural feeling for a man.'

And the quick shot straight from the hip to the shoulder just so long and long enough, almost a snap-shot from my 270 Weatherby that folded the wildebeest at 305 yards, my boy paced it, the meat sweet and clean. If your wildebeest runs even three yards after the hit the glandular juices of stress spoil the meat. The meat *stinks* of fear and death. The guests start back from the barbecue pit appalled.

'*Qu'elle est cette bête morte?*'

'What is this dead beast?'

This was a fearless kill. It would yield up brave steaks. And this was a joy too but a different joy, steadier, quieter, the joy of a craftsman in his trade. Joy that leaves a man fresh inside like the smell of salt spray and the smell of valor in the bull ring . . .

'S'Death what stuff's here?'

The *Snows of Kilimanjaro* was certainly the best if not the only writing Hemingway ever did. It is one of the best stories in the language about death, the *stink* of death. You know the writer has been there and brought it back. The end deserves a place among the great passages of English prose, with the end of Joyce's *The Dead* and the end of *The Great Gatsby*. The pilot was pointing: 'White white white as far as the eye could see ahead, the snows of Kilimanjaro.' And a blinding flash of white must have been the last thing Papa saw when he put the double-barrel 12-gauge shotgun against his forehead and tripped both triggers.

So Papa sold death to Hollywood when he let them tack a happy ending onto their dreadful movie of *The Snows of Kilimanjaro*. Instead of the phantom messenger of death who appears at the end of the story, a real live shitting pilot from Hollywood arrives with penicillin — just the thing for a writer's gangrene. And Papa sat and watched this butchery and signed his name to it.

'Look, they're gone!' says wifey pointing to where the vultures had been roosting. Yes even the vultures have flapped away in disgust from that sell out.

On a sell-out you have to think in terms of *properties*. I mean he sells *The Snows of Kilimanjaro* which is gilt-edged stuff for *The Green Hills of Africa*. Was *The Green Hills* even worth doing? No. For all that hunting and loading shit I'd rather read *Field and Stream* and *The American Rifleman*. But the real tragedy is that *The Snows of Kilimanjaro* could have been a great film about Death. Hemingway could smell death on others. Here he is in a jeep with General Lanham, known as Bucky to his friends, and Ernie was a real general lover. It's worse than being a cop lover.

'Have to relieve that man,' says Bucky.

'Bucky,' says Ernie, 'You won't have to relieve him. He won't make it. He stinks of death.'

When the jeep reached Regimental Command Post it was stopped by Lieutenant Colonel John Ruggles.

'General . . .' said Ruggles saluting. 'The Major has just been killed. Who takes the First Battalion?'

And there is a great description in *Farewell to Arms* of the feeling you get when leaving the body at death. He has an opportunity to do a film about his *specialty* the thing he *does best* as a writer. And he throws it away for an expensive hunting trip. So the writer doesn't die after all. He will go back to America and hole up in a cabin he knows about in Minnesota and write the great American novel. His gear is packed. The jeep will come at dawn. The sun is setting. The wise old hunter lights his pipe and points with the burning firebrand to the white dome of Kilimanjaro.

'Don't ever sell your dream, son.' The old hunter waves to the jeep. 'You see he had learned that life is more important than death. He had learned to live humbly for something he believed in. I guess it was just making his own dream real for a lot of people. You see Ernie wanted to *give*, he wanted to give from the heart with every word he wrote.'

He's gonna pay death off with a load of corn, or so he thinks.

    'You reckon ill who leave me out
    When me you fly I am the wings.'

Who wrote that? I mean Death was Ernie's inspiration. When Death walked out on him in Hollywood he took Ernie's inspiration with him. 'It doesn't come anymore,' he groans. You have to respect him for the courage to blow his brains out like that, don't care what you say about the higher courage of living, it takes guts to do that. Makes me feel queasy just to think about it. He certainly died in style.

'I reckon you could have put your foot in the back of his head where the two barrels of heavy duck load splattered out even if it was a medium-sized foot and you didn't want to put it there.'

Old Lady: It must be very dangerous to be a writer.

Papa: It is Madam, and few survive it.

Does the book contain memorable passages? I first read Denton Welch in 1948. I re-read *Maiden Voyage* thirty years later and found that I had virtually memorized passages from the book. I have already quoted an example concerning his 'horrible little black pony, its awful yellow teeth.'

And here is the end of *The Great Gatsby*: 'He had come a long way to this blue lawn and his dream must have seemed so close that he could hardly fail to grasp it. Gatsby believed in the green light, the orgastic future that year by year recedes before us. It eluded us then, but that's no matter, tomorrow we will run faster, stretch out our arms further and one fine morning... So we beat on, boats against the current, borne back ceaselessly into the past.'

This passage stays with the reader and becomes part of his inner landscape 'commensurate with his capacity for wonder.'

And the characters? Can you see them? So long as there are readers Gatsby will look across his blue lawn to the green light at the end of Daisy's dock. But I can't see the protagonist of *Appointment in Samarra*. I can't remember his name. He is as real and as quickly forgotten as today's newspaper: Elderly Woman Dies in Fire. Death was attributed to smoke inhalation. Why should this elderly woman thrust her death upon one? I doubt if she even made a good-looking corpse.

Does the writer play fair with the reader? There are rules to this game between reader and writer. Two books are on the list simply to illustrate the violation of the rules.

The Critical Threshold by Brian Stableford. Colonists stranded on a distant planet undergo an alteration through contact with a powerful hallucinogenic substance given off by mating butterflies. The change leaves them devoid of language and so altered that the human rescue party inspires in them horrors and something akin to nausea. A very interesting idea, but the writer couldn't follow through. We never find out what this wondrous change consists of. We are led to expect something that is not forthcoming.

In *The Great Sun Flower* by Clifford Stone, the protagonist has a *strange* experience in Nice. He won't talk about it. So this *experience* which leads to his madness and suicide by hanging is never revealed to the reader. It's like a who-done-it where you don't find out who done it or a monster movie where you never get to see the monster. It's just the old 'Nothing will ever bring me to reveal what I saw in that infamous crypt...' (where the inventiveness of the writer lies buried).

What about the title? Does it arouse your interest? Does it evoke a picture in your mind? A good title can sell a mediocre book, a bad title can sink a good book. *The Biological Time Bomb* is a much more informative book than *Future Shock*. *Future Shock* became a best seller on the title, while *The*

Biological Time Bomb sank into oblivion. There were two hundred suggested titles for *Jaws*.

Devise alternative endings: Happy endings like Papa used to make. Gatsby marries Daisy and here they are twenty years later living in the south of France a dreary empty snobbish couple. Daisy has become a secret drunk.

'Looking for this, Daisy?' He holds up a bottle of gin. Quarrelling, angling for invitations to the Duchess's party.

Lord Jim lives on to become a living legend written up in all the Sunday Supplements, living in a 19th-century set that could fold tomorrow. Jim points sadly to graffiti scrawled on the wall of his compound: *Honky Honk Home.* He should be gone with the wild geese in the sick smell of morning. Often an early death is the kindest gift a writer can bestow on a beloved character, and Gatsby and Lord Jim both shimmer and glow from the love bestowed upon them by their creators.

You can move character and story to another time and place, always looking for the right slot where it can fit. Conrad's *Heart of Darkness* becomes *Apocalypse Now.* In the early days of the Vietnam conflict CIA agents set up their Ops in remote outposts, requisitioned private armies, overawed the super-stitious natives and achieved the status of white Gods. So the context of 19th-century colonialism was briefly duplicated. That is what writing is about: time travel. So I drafted Denton Welch to be the protagonist of a 19th-century western on which I was then working.*

In this novel Kim Carson is hiding out in a remote mountain valley with nothing to occupy his mind except an anthology of poetry, leather-bound with gilt edges and this leads us to an exercise I call *intersection reading*. Just where and under what circumstances did you read? What were you reading when the phone rang or some other interruption occurred? Note the exact place in your reading where this occurred. The point at which your stream of consciousness — and when you read of course you are simply borrowing the writer's stream of it, being bored by your own, if indeed you *have* one, isn't it all just bits and pieces, shreds and patches? Constantly being cut by *seemingly* random factors which on examination turn out to be highly significant and appropriate. For example, I am walking down a New York Street, Elizabeth Street come to think of it, just turned off Houston past The Volunteers of America. I am thinking about New Mexico and I look up and there is a New

* *The Place of Dead Roads.*

Mexico license plate. Land of Enchantment. So note and write down in the margin actual interruptions, which may be frequent if you are riding on a subway. I admire the intrepid breed of subway readers; perhaps they are quite literally escaping into their books. I have never heard of a reader being attacked. Why only yesterday a black youth was occupying a double seat with such truculent insolence that no one, myself included, dared to demand our squatters rights, but a young man with a large book on mathematics, he was very technical, made the sullen youth move his briefcase and set right to work on his formulae. So choose the subway for really *adventurous* intersections, but waiting rooms and airports are also rich motherlodes. You can just sit there and attract incidents like a blue serge suit attracts lint.

And trains are the best because you're perfectly safe and some oaf won't suddenly confront you with a bestial snarl: 'Who are you reading at?'

I just tried an interesting experiment. I turn on the TV, open an anthology of poetry and read a few lines, noting action and words on screen. I throw away some duds but the hits are impressive. Just try it.

'A violet by a mossy stone half hidden from the eye.' Wordsworth/*Lucy poems*. There's a flower on screen right now.

'How dull it is to make an end/ to rust unburnished not to shine in use.' Tennyson/*Ulysses*. On screen a cowhand is explaining to the girl he doesn't want to be *tied down*. He wants to keep moving like a tumbleweed.

'And never lifted up a single stone.' Wordsworth/*Michael*. On screen some woman is rubbing on her hand cream. No stone lifting for her.

'For sweetest things turn sour by their deeds/ and lilies that fester smell far worse than weeds.' Shakespeare. On screen a personable model extols some kinda toothpaste called POL makes your breath soul-kissing sweet.

'The same bourgeois magic wherever the mail train sets you down.' Rimbaud/*Historic Evening*. A documentary on screen shows computerized travel at Kennedy Airport.

'And the dream fades...' Rimbaud/*Vigils*. On screen the lights in the Empire State Building go out.

'The clouds gathered over the seas formed of an eternity of hot tears.' Rimbaud/*Childhood*. On screen Arthur Miller is relating the death of this magnificent old salesman who died while trying to sell some shit or other over the phone.

44

'Death will come when thou art dead . . . soon soon.'
Shelley/*To Night*. News story about some psycho tried to
strangle a black man in a hospital. Seems this same Perp had
shot two other black victims and cut their hearts out and taken
their hearts away with him.

What do we conclude from this exercise? It seems like our
entire sensory input is pre-programmed. Mektoub. It is written.
Snip. Snip. Cut it up.

You can imagine a context. Say you are reading this in some
19th century jungle outpost. Your traitorous boys slink away
into the night. 'Ali! Mustapha! Where are you?' You ready your
submachine gun and settle down to read to the pulsing signal
drums. How sleep the brave/ REDRUM REDRUM
REDRUM the drums pulse. 'Sounds like they got Red and a
rottener bastard never drew a breath. By Allah their country's
wishes blast . . .

'Just doing our job is all. Recollect in the Congo they have a
bounty on Niggers you turn in a pair of ears and collect. But it
turns out some do-gooder bleeding heart bounty hunters was
just cutting off the ears and letting the nigger go to undermine
the whole purpose of the program. So after that you had to turn
in his plumbing, cock and balls. And Red used to sit there
counting the pricks and handing out the gold. But who am I
to be critical with a fishing creel full waiting on the line?'
'And freedom shall a while repair to dwell a weeping hermit
there . . .'

Fire arrows rain on the roof.

Or maybe you are a sixteen year old prep school boy on
vacation Tausnitch edition *Pension in Cannes*.

    'There's not a joy in the world can give like that it takes
        away.
    When bloom of early thought declines in feelings dull
        decay.'   Byron.

The world weary burnt out look is irresistably attractive to
the young and innocent.

    'Shredded incense in a cloud
    From closet long to quiet vowed
    Moldering her lute and books among
    AS WHEN A QUEEN long dead was young.'
                                      Browning.

The boy thinks this is funny and camps around with a skull
mask he will wear tonight at the costume party at the Villa

Mauresque where the big writer lives and isn't he lucky to have wangled an invitation through his uncle in the State Department. How he will astonish them! He has the poem printed on a T shirt with skeleton ribs and he will act it all out like a charade. Some way the Villa Mauresque will be the 'closet long to quiet vowed' out of which he will *burst* 'as when A QUEEN!!!' Long dead . . . he puts on his skull mask. Now he nonchalantly strips off his skeleton tights and his rib shirt and stands there chewing gum in his insouciant dazzling youth. 'Was young' is written across his chest in gilt letters. It was all very tasteful Audrey thought . . .

So here is Kim Carson in his remote hideout reading poems over and over. Verses trill and tinkle from icy streams.

> 'and the stars that oversprinkle
> all the heavens seem to twinkle
> with a crystalline delight.' Poe.

Holding the fish by its tail and its head Kim bites into the back of an eight inch trout. Verses whisper and sigh from grass and leaves. Kim is thinking about Tom's recent death in an ambush arranged by a certain bounty hunter named Mike Chase. Account to settle. Book keeping he called it. 'Rolled round in earth's diurnal course with rocks and stones and trees.' Wordsworth.

This blank assertion of the finality of death and human mortality from the man who wrote *Intimations of Immortality*? Wordsworth like so many artists was an *alien*, Kim decided, an *immortal* alien feeling the estrangement of human mortality. 'Old unhappy far off things and battle long ago.'

He could see Lucy poems written across the evening sky. 'Fair as a star when only one is shining in the sky.' Kim looks up at the evening star his hands bloody from cleaning fish. Who was this little twist? Was there some sordid English scene behind this, panted out behind the cow shed?

'Don't tell your mother and I'll give ye half a crown.'

This struck Kim as unlikely. She was a phantom like Wordsworth the English Bard with his walking stick and his black slouchy poet hat and cape and his 'Dewy fingers cold/ returned to deck her hallowed mould.' (Collins) These creepy old English poets!

She was a phantom of *delight*, a hot English fox maiden fat, mate for a ghostly man of letters self-invoked to haunt 'This heath this calm this quiet scene/ the memory of what has been/ and never more will be . . .'

Kim sees flashes of his life with Tom like postcards: 'Having fine time. Wish you were here.'

Adding the Lucy poems to our list. There is a literary mystery here. Who killed the poet's phantom nymphet? Who drew the gradual dusky veil on Lucy. Did the poet sacrifice mortal love for immortal verse?

I think of this reading list as an organic accretion designed to animate works of excellence or distinction in some capacity. I intend to assemble from the list anthologies of outstanding passages not subdivided into Death/Love/Solitude/Old Age, but arranged by associational affinity.

There is a fish that lives in very deep water in perpetual darkness. During the mating game the male becomes physically attached to the female and slowly she absorbs him until only his testicle protrudes from the female body.

'The Lord turned and looked at Kim. His face was immeasurably old, smooth and yellow like flexible amber incrusted with layers of cruelty and evil and abominations that stopped the breath and closed round Kim's heart with a soft slimy clutch. The eyes were shafts of dead water leading down into black depths.'

There are panoramas of sunsets and sunrises and of course eventually the anthologies will be illustrated with reproductions of paintings and photographs. You're just nobody if you're not on *the list*. Wearily our reader sweeps a pile of best-sellers to the floor as a Michelin inspector is said to have dismissed an unsuccessful soufflé. Oh yes, we will have our inspectors.

The Inspector is a shabby gray inconspicuous man. He glances around the vernissage and yawns. He identifies himself. The artist and the gallery owner stand there waiting. He shakes his head with a terrible smile. The List will grow into an institute with a research staff, a library, a museum and film archives. Bulletins will be issued and funds allotted to deserving projects.

Ten Years and a Billion Dollars

My general theory since 1971 has been that the Word is literally a virus, and that it has not been recognized as such because it has achieved a state of relatively stable symbiosis with its human host; that is to say, the Word Virus (the Other Half) has established itself so firmly as an accepted part of the human organism that it can now sneer at gangster viruses like smallpox and turn them in to the Pasteur Institute. But the Word clearly bears the single identifying feature of virus: it is an organism with no internal function other than to replicate itself.

I asked some of my Buddhist friends, including Allen Ginsberg, this simple question: who are you actually talking to when you are 'talking to yourself'? Without presuming a complete understanding of the nature of the Word, I suggested that such an understanding would make it possible to shut off the internal dialogue, to rub out the Word. Allen replied that the Buddhists have developed techniques over the centuries to do just that; it may be so. Not having experimented with their techniques, I can't say. But I wanted some *answers*, and it seems to me that in the three thousand years the Buddhists have had to toss this around, they have not come up with any. I offered this challenge then and I repeat it now: give me ten years and a billion dollars for research, and I'll get some *answers* to the question of Word.

But I do not have a billion dollars, and I may or may not have ten years, so in the meantime I have developed certain techniques of my own. First of all, I recognized writing as a magical operation, and since such operations are designed to produce specific results, this leads us to an inquiry as to the purposes of writing. Remember that the written word is an image; that the first writing was pictorial, and so painting and writing were at one time a single operation. Historically, they do not separate until we have a highly stylized pictorial writing, as in Egyptian, which of course developed much later. The original invention from which writing developed was quite simply to create on a cave wall images and scenes: hunting, and often so-called pornographic drawings. The purpose was originally ceremonial or magical, and when the work is separated from its magical function, it loses vitality. That is, when some tribe starts making dolls for the tourists, it's gone. And that is what bestsellers are doing — whole valleys of dolls and shark teeth for the tourists. It may make money but it isn't magical. I know Dali says the measure of genius is gold, and I agree that artists should be at least as well-paid as plumbers.

Journalism is closer to the magical origins of writing than most fiction. That is, at least a few operators in this area — people like the late Hearst and Henry Luce — certainly quite clearly and consciously saw journalism as a magical operation designed to bring about certain effects. And the technology is the technology of magic; in the case of newspapers and magazines, mostly black magic. They stick pins in someone's image and then show that image to millions of people. You can see how easy it is, if you own a newspaper, to start slipping in non-existent events; this has been and is being done all the time — by TIME especially, in fact. Starting with being a week ahead, they literally write the news before it happens; which is why they print so many false statements that they have to retract. And so you get a retraction from them — how many people read the retraction compared to the number who have read the falsified story? You have all heard this one: a story went out that some hippies tripping on LSD stared at the sun and went blind. Later there was a retraction — the story was a hoax. But more people saw the story than saw the retraction, so the story is still circulating and still believed.

William Randolph Hearst had two house rules at San Simeon: One, everybody staying in Mr Hearst's house must appear at dinner no matter what condition he or she is in. That's very understandable — otherwise people would be goofing off in their rooms, imitating his mannerisms, and he would lose control of the situation. It's the old Army game of Roll Call. And rule number two: nobody may mention the word DEATH in Mr Hearst's presence. There is a very good magical reason for that rule. Mr Hearst was playing Death. Playing Death means you must always be able to affect others, but they may never be allowed to affect you. Someone comes down to dinner in a skeleton suit, the old man could lose his position.

So what is the difference between Hearst and a writer of fiction? I mean a real writer, like Beckett, Genet, Joyce, Hemingway, Conrad, Fitzgerald, Kafka... right away we have a distinction: can you imagine a writer or an artist who would be afraid to hear the word DEATH? I sure can't. Any writer who cannot hear that word is not a writer. It can only mean one thing: he is trying to play Death and is not sure of his credentials, like a fake cop doesn't want to see a real one. Another distinction is responsibility. Genet says that a writer assumes the terrible burden of responsibility for the characters he creates. They are his creations and he is responsible for them. Journalists on the other hand have no responsibility whatever for the characters they create. Let them go and hijack a plane, kill five women in Arizona, assassinate the President, and what happens to them after that? Who cares? A basic difference in attitude.

I have given my students several exercises to sharpen their perception as writers and to help them make their own enquiries into the nature of word and image as they manifest themselves along association lines. The exercise that has elicited the greatest response and produced the most interesting results has been the Walk Exercise. Basically it consists in taking a walk with the continuity and perceptions you encounter. The original version of this exercise was taught me by an old Mafia Don in Columbus, Ohio: seeing everyone on the street before he sees you. Do this for a while in any neighbourhood, and you will soon meet other players who are doing the same thing. Generally speaking, if you see other people before they see you, they *won't* see you. I have even managed to get past a whole block of guides and shoeshine boys in Tangier this way, thus earning my Moroccan monicker: 'El Hombre Invisible'. Another version of this exercise is simply to give no one a reason to look at you. Sooner or later, however, someone will see you. Try to guess why he saw you — what were you thinking when he saw your face?

Another exercise that is very effective is walking on colors. Pick out all the reds on a street, focusing only on red objects — brick, lights, sweaters, signs. Shift to green, blue, orange, yellow. Notice how the colors begin to stand out more sharply of their own accord. I was walking on yellow when I saw a yellow amphibious jeep near the corner of 94th Street and Central Park West. It was called the Thing. This reminded me of the Thing I knew in Mexico. He was nearly seven feet tall and had played the Thing in a horror movie of the same name, and everybody called him the Thing. I hadn't thought about the Thing in twenty years, and would not have thought about him except walking on yellow at that particular moment.

Immediately the story of a horrible Mexican weekend came back to me, as related by Kells Elvins. Kells, his wife, and the Thing had been invited to the country house of a rich Mexican, and looking forward to swimming pools, luxury, good food and drinks, they inadvisedly accepted. They arrived at a barren stone castle with hardly a stick of furniture, where drunken-machos — muy macho much man, also much son-of-bitch — were blasting at terrified cats with pearl-handled .45's while the cats ran around and around trying to escape, which they couldn't do because the doors were locked — bullets ricocheting all over the castle. Much more dangerous to the human spectators than to the cats, who were smaller and moving much faster. That .45 is one of the most inaccurate handguns in circulation, and the machos were crazy drunk, so of course Kells and his wife and the Thing were in favor of an immediate withdrawal, but found they were locked in like the cats. The machos — five foot six in elevator shoes — hated the Thing because he was taller. So they held him at gunpoint and took turns spitting drinks in his face.

This scene and many others from Mexico — 1950 Mexico City College — flashed through my mind like a film; some pictures dim and grainy, others in technicolor — all triggered by the amphibious yellow jeep.

And I was reminded of a description I read of the old Tong Wars in New York's Chinatown, where the Chinese gunmen would squat down in the Bloody Angle of Doyers Street in front of the Chinese Light Lutheran Church with their Colt .45 revolvers, shut both eyes tight, and blast away until the gun was empty. So those old bullets were whistling all up and down the street.

'Light Lutherans — for an instant I'm at the door of the Baptist Church on St. John's Island in the West Indies. White paint buckles and peels from the walls. I smell the fruit and the sugar and the heat, then a long tight funnel of New York wind sucks me back to today.' (This is a quote from a student in my 1974 writing class at C.C.N.Y.) When you take these walks you are literally travelling in time along association lines.

So late the next afternoon I took a walk in Chinatown, and here is what I saw . . . a whitish wash of winter sunlight afternoon pale through a slot in the buildings blood splotched on his white shirt and overalls he appears not to connect with the ground or anything else . . . he shifts his eyes right and then left

51

and suspicious yellow rays emanate from his too-old interior . . . cold and windy outside as I enter through the turnstile another guy exits his hair and jowly face a medium gray *la via del tren subterraneo esta peligrosa* obey the police I haven't been in New York long don't touch that cat you'll catch something hey honey want to ditch your wife guess Chinese do like pork look at feet only a good way to travel he holds the images of sterility and puts himself outside of what he wants with a sharp knowing glance and surreptitious eyeballs — I can push him onto the tracks flirting around the horny bastard keeps staring at my face or hair or crotch diamonds are still a girl's best friend can I have a quarter? the film had too much violence stand clear of the moving platform oh yes there's so much to learn in Chinese kitchen next door last gravy running out look they died years ago the coats and people a blur the wind is slamming signs around clattering debris in an empty lot of dusty window pants for sale piss in a black puddle against a stone corner I was embarrassed what if someone sees me blue jeans leering at me intimately you wonder how I can know how you feel perhaps there are no complete strangers . . .

The word is a virus.

It Belongs to the Cucumbers

It seems that tape recordings made with no apparent input have turned up unexplained voices on the tape. 'Voice phenomena are done with a tape recorder and microphones set up in the usual way and using factory-fresh tapes. No sounds are heard or emitted during the recording, but on replay faint voices of unknown origin appear to have been recorded.' (*The Handbook of Psychic Discoveries*, Ostrander & Schroeder 1975.) Visible speech diagrams and voiceprints have confirmed that these actually are recorded voices. The most complete source book is *Breakthrough*, by Konstantin Raudive (Taplinger Publishing Co., 1971).

These voices seem an appropriate topic to take up at the Kerouac School of Disembodied Poetics. Before discussing the experiments carried out by Raudive, I will describe experiments performed with Brion Gysin and Ian Sommerville twelve years before *Breakthrough* was published and in fact before it was written. These experiments started not on tape recorders but on paper. In 1959 Brion Gysin said 'Writing is fifty years behind painting' and applied the montage technique to words on a page. These cut-up experiments appeared in *Minutes To Go*, in 1959.

Subsequently we cut up the Bible, Shakespeare, Rimbaud, our own writing, anything in sight. We made thousands of cut-ups. When you cut and rearrange words on a page, new words emerge. And words change meaning. The word 'drafted', as into the Army, moved into a context of blueprints or contracts, gives an altered meaning. New words and altered meanings are implicit in the process of cutting up, and could have been anticipated. Other results were not expected. When you experiment with cut-ups over a period of time, some of the cut and rearranged texts seem to refer to future events. I cut up an article written by John Paul Getty and got: 'It is a bad thing to sue your own father.' And a year later one of his sons did sue him. In 1964 I made a cut-up and got what seemed at the time a totally inexplicable phrase: 'And here is a horrid air conditioner.' in 1974 I moved into a loft with a broken air conditioner which was removed to put in a new unit. And there was three hundred pounds of broken air conditioner on my floor — a horrid disposal problem, heavy and solid, emerged from a cut-up ten years ago.

The next step was cut-ups on the tape recorder. Brion was the first to take this obvious step. The first tape recorder cut-ups were a simple extension of cut-ups on paper. You record, say, ten minutes on the recorder. Then you spin the reel backwards or forwards without recording. Stop at random and cut in a phrase. How random is random? We know so much that we don't consciously know we know, that perhaps the cut-in was not random. Of course this procedure on the tape recorder produces new words by altered juxtaposition just as new words are produced by cut-ups on paper.

We went on to exploit the potentials of the tape-recorder: cut up, slow down, speed up, run backwards, inch the tape, play several tracks at once, cut back and forth between two recorders. As soon as you start experimenting with slowdowns, speedups, overlays, etc., you will get new words that were not on the original recordings. There are then many ways of producing words and voices on tape that did not get there by the usual recording procedure, words and voices that are quite definitely and clearly recognizable by a consensus of listeners. I have gotten words and voices from barking dogs. No doubt one could do much better with dolphins. And words will emerge from recordings of dripping faucets. In fact, almost any sound that is not too uniform may produce words. 'Every little breeze seems to whisper Louise . . . The very tree branches brushing against her window seemed to mutter *murder murder murder*.' Well, the branches may have muttered just that, and you could hear it back with a recorder. Everything you hear and see is there for you to hear and see it.

Some time ago a young man came to see me and said he was going mad. Street signs, overheard conversations, radio broadcasts, seemed to refer to him in some way. I told him 'Of course they refer to you. *You* see and hear them.' Years ago, Ian Sommerville, Stewart Gordon, and your reporter had turned into the rue des Vignes, just off the Place de France in Tangier. Walking ahead of us was a middle-aged Arab couple, obviously poor country people down from the mountains. And one turned to the other and said: 'WHAT ARE YOU GOING TO DO?' We all heard it. Perhaps the Arab words just happened to sound like that. Perhaps it was a case of consensual scanning. I had a friend who went 'mad' in Tangier. He was scanning out personal messages from Arab broadcasts. This is the more subjective phenomenon of personal scanning patterns. I say 'more' rather than pose the either/or subjective/objective alternative, since all phenomena are both subjective *and* objective. He was, after all, listening to radio broadcasts.

Now to consider Raudive's experimental procedure. The experiments were carried out in a soundproof studio. A new blank tape was turned on and allowed to record. Then the tape was played back, the experimenter listening through headphones, and quite recognizable voices and words were found to be recorded on the tape. Raudive has recorded 100,000 phrases of these voices. The speech is almost double the usual speed, and the sound is pulsed in rhythms like poetry or chanting. These voices are in a number of accents and languages, often quite ungrammatical... 'You I friends. Where stay?' sounds like a Tangier hustler. Reading through the sample voices in *Breakthrough*, I was struck by many instances of a distinctive style reminiscent of schizophrenic speech, certain dream utterances, some of the cut-ups and delirium voices like the last words of Dutch Schultz. Many of the voices allegedly come from the dead. Hitler, Nietzsche, Goethe, Jesus Christ, anybody who is anybody is there, many of them having undergone a marked deterioration of their mental and artistic faculties. Goethe isn't what he used to be. Hitler had a bigger and better mouth when he was alive. On one level the recorded voices procedure is a form of sophisticated electronic table-tapping, and table-tapping is one aspect of the cut-up experiments I have described. What better way to contact someone than to cut and rearrange his actual words? Certainly an improvement on the usual scene where Shakespeare is announced, to be followed by some excruciatingly bad poetry. Whether there is actual contact with the dead is an academic question so long as there is no way to prove or disprove it.

I have pointed out a stylistic similarity between the voices recorded by Raudive, dream speech, schizophrenic speech, words spoken in delirium, and cut-ups. This does not apply to all the material in these categories, much of which may be quite banal and undistinguished. For example, a frequently recurring phrase in Raudive's book is 'Heat the bathroom, company is coming.' This is no esoteric code, but simply refers to a Latvian custom. When they are expecting guests, someone goes into the bathroom and lights the stove. It is a question of selecting material which is stylistically interesting, or which may contain references of personal or prophetic significance. Here are some examples of dream speech: from my own dream diaries:

'We can come out when shadows cover the cracks. You need black money here. We still don't have the nouns. Do you like to get lost or patrol cars? The symbol of the skull and the symbol of soap turn on the same axis. Can't you keep any ice? The Inspectorate of Canada is banging on the door. I suppose you think Missouri is a lump. You have an airforce appetite. The lair of the bear is in Chicago. The unconscious imitated by cheesecake. A tin of tomato soup in Arizona. Where naked troubadours shoot snotty baboons. Green is a man to fill is a boy. I can take the hut set anywhere. A book called *Advanced Outrage*. An astronaut named Platt. First American shot on Mrs. Life is a flickering shadow with violence before and after it. A good loser always gives up control for what the situation would be if control wasn't there to look around in it.'

And here are two examples of dream slang: an ounce of heroin is a 'beach'. 'To camel' is dream slang for 'fuck'. Unfortunately I do not have at hand any examples of schizophrenic speech. I remember only two: 'Doctorhood is being made with me.' Stylistically similar to the Inspectorate of Canada. And: 'Radius radius .. it is enough.'

Here are some phrases from Raudive's book. I have taken these phrases out of what might be called minimal context for purposes of illustration: 'Cheers here are the nondead. Here are the cunning ones. We are here because of you. We are all longing to go home. Politics, here is death. Take the grave with you. It snows horribly. We see Tibet with the binoculars of the people. Give reinforcement. Diminish the stopper. Sometimes only the native country loves. I am expensive. We are coordinated, the guard is manifold. You belong probably to the cucumbers. Telephone with restraint comrade. It is difficult in Train A. Covering fire. Send orders. Are you without jewelry? A lecture is taking place here. We have become accustomed to our sick ones. Get out of the defensive position. Speed is required. Leave it in full gear. Have done with the seemingly apparent. Please to use studio postulated to you. Faustus, good morning. I demand our authorities. This is the aunt's language. Identity card. It is permitted. A pistol is our man. This is operational. Even the wolves do not stay here. Into battle. The long life flees. We ignite. It is bad here. Here the birds burn. It smells of the operational death. Knowledgeable Goth, the deed of the future. Believe. Separated. Here is eternity. The far away exists. You are the contract. Are in salt? We have been looking all over the place for human beings. Ah good the sea. Professor of non-existence, the body is evidence of the spirit. The natural key. We are the language here. The doctor is on the market. Good evening our chap, are you making mummies to standard? It is enough. Reason submitted. Called at a bad time. This is operational even in the middle. With binoculars at the border, you have nevertheless to fetch our clothes. Prepare trousers in the bathroom. Why are you a German? Clean out the earth. The new Germany. Hitler is a good animal-infesting louse. Have you stolen horses with him? *Yo siento*. Man pricks. *Buena cosa* man. Draw the spirit to the *plata*. Hurry to make the flutes. Facts see us. I am practically here. A good crossing. The earth disintegrated.'

Commentary: 'We see Tibet with the binoculars of the people.' In 1970, about the time that these recordings were made, I wrote a story about a Chinese patrol which finds a Tibetan monastery taken over by the CIA to test a radioactive virus ... 'Yen Lee studied the village through his field glasses ...'

'You belong probably to the cucumbers.' I don't know how many of you are familiar with a term used to designate the CIA: 'the pickle factory.' 'He works for the pickle factory' means he is a CIA man. I think this designation was mentioned in TIME or NEWSWEEK. Well, pickles are made from cucumbers, so it doesn't seem too far-fetched to postulate that 'cucumbers' refers to the CIA.

'Telephone with restraint comrade.' Watch what you say over the phone — the cucumbers are listening in.

'Are you without jewelry?' May refer to lasers, which are made with jewels.

'Bind death — Obey death.' Compare to Dutch Schultz's last words, 'I don't want harmony. I want harmony.'

'Are you in salt? We have been looking all over the place for human beings.' Salt could refer to any basic commodity. In this case, since the voices are discarnate, the reference is probably to human bodies. Your blood as you know has the saline content of sea water, — 'Ah good the sea.' Now, to say 'Are you in blood?' would blow the vampiric cover.

'Have you stolen horses with him?' Is a German proverb

meaning 'Can you trust him?'

'Draw the spirit to the *plata*.' Raudive considers this utterance inexplicable. Apparently he did not know that *plata* is a general Spanish slang term for money.

'A good crossing. The earth disintegrated.' Some years ago scientists drew up a plan for a space ship to be propelled by atomic blasts behind it. Well, that would be a motive for blowing up the earth: propulsion to healthier areas.

The publication of *Breakthrough* in England caused quite a stir. One of the editors, Peter Bander, later published a book entitled *Voices From the Tapes*, describing the reactions in England. There were articles in the press, radio and television programs, much discussion pro and con. Some people protested that if these are voices from the dead, they seem to be living not in celestial realms but in a cosmic hell. In consequence the voices may be misleading, interested, even downright ill-intentioned. Well, what did they expect? A chorus of angels with tips on the stock market? Others protested that contact with these voices is dangerous, citing the use of black magic and the invocation of lower astral entities by Nazi leaders. An article written by a psychic researcher, Gordon Turner, typifies the 'dangerous for the uninitiated' line. Turner's article was written in answer to an article by someone named Cass, in which Cass said: 'If a door has been opened between this world and the next, then the masses, armed with their cheap transistor sets and five-pound Hong Kong recorders, will participate despite Gordon Turner, the Pope, and the Government.'

Here is Turner: 'I believe *Breakthrough* should not have been published. Does (Cass) think it is safe for anyone and everyone to open themselves to this kind of influence? Has he the slightest conception of how dangerous this might be?' Dangerous to whom exactly? When people start talking about the danger posed by making psychic knowledge available to the masses, they are generally trying to monopolize this knowledge for themselves. In my opinion, the best safeguard against the abuse of such knowledge is widespread dissemination. The more people that know about it, the better.

Raudive considers three theories to account for the voices: 1) They are somehow imprinted on the tape by electromagnetic energy generated by the unconscious minds of the researchers or people connected with them. 2) The voices are of extra-terrestrial origin. 3) The voices come from the dead. He then crosses out Number 1, the imprint theory, because it is 'technically impossible.' It seems to me that we are operating in an area where technical impossibilities, in terms of what we know about magnetic tape and the way in which sounds and voices are imprinted by the usual means, no longer apply.

Remember that your memory bank contains tapes of everything you have ever heard, including of course your own words. Press a certain button, and a news broadcast you heard ten years ago plays back. Under hypnosis, people have remembered in detail conversations and events that took place many years ago, and this has been confirmed by witnesses. Hypnotic subjects have been able to recall exactly what doctors and nurses said during an operation, and such recall, particularly if it has a menacing or derogatory content, can be extremely disturbing . . .

'One thing is sure — he don't look good.'

'A filthy mess . . .'

'Sew her up, it's inoperable.'

'Clamps, nurse, he's bleeding like a pig.'

'Prepare the patient for a heart shot.'

'A round of drinks he dies on the table.'

These irresponsible observations are recorded and stored in the patient's memory bank, enough so to convey a permanent patient status. In Esquire's 1971 Christmas issue, there was an article called 'Future Shock'; Doctor Cheek, who carried out hypnotic experiments on post-operative subjects and found they were recording every word and sound in the operating room, recommended that silence be observed during an operation. Because what the patient hears during an operation is filed with all his tapes of pain, fear, helplessness and hostility — all the horrible, frightening, disgusting things he has ever known awake or asleep, conscious or unconscious, from his conception.

Everyone you have ever known, however briefly, is there on film and tape. Take a look at these talking films and you will begin to notice that certain words and characters tend to recur. The rude clerk in Hong Kong bore a strong resemblance to the rude clerk in New York, and both used the same words to indicate they did not have what you asked for: 'I never heard of it.'

The more you look at it, the more it looks like a tired old film, nice voices nasty voices, good guys and bad guys, the old game of war from the Stone Age to eternity . . .

'Are we men or toothless crones? How long will we allow the filthy Zambesi to plunder our fishing territories?

'As free men we cannot stand idly by.' Time to get yourself hid good and the deeper the better. 'And I say to Russia, beware the fury of a patient man.' A good crossing. The earth disintegrated. Old war tapes. We all have millions of hours of it, even if we never fired a gun. War tapes, hate tapes, fear tapes, pain tapes, happy tapes, sad tapes, funny tapes, all stirring around in a cement mixer of voices.

Raudive dismisses the second alternative explanation for the origin of the voices — that they are extraterrestrial — because they are 'too banal'. Well, no reason to think we have a monopoly on banality. His reasoning exemplifies the error of either/or thinking. Having categorically crossed out 1) and 2), he is stuck with Number 3: the voices come from the dead. I could suggest other possible explanations: the voices are a backplay of recordings stored in the memory banks of the experimenters.

Now the psychiatrists tell us that any voices anyone hears in his head originate there, and that they do not and cannot have an extraneous origin. The whole psychiatric dogma that voices are the imaginings of a sick mind has been called into question by voices which are of extraneous origin and are objectively and demonstrably there on tape. So the psychotic patients may be tuning in to a global and intergalactic network of voices, some using quite sophisticated electronic equipment. It belongs probably to the cucumbers. Fifteen years ago in Norway, experiments indicated that voices could be projected directly into the brain of the subject by an electromagnetic field around the head. The experiments were in a formative stage at that time. So maybe we are all walking around under a magnetic dome of prerecorded word and image, and Raudive and the other experimenters are simply plugging into the prerecording.

Could you, by your cutting up, overlaying, scrambling, cut and nullify the prerecordings of your own future? Could the whole prerecorded future of the human race be nullified or altered? I don't know — let's see. And don't let any smooth old voices ease you out of it . . . 'There are certain things my son that human beings are not permitted to know —' *like what we are doing* — 'Son you'd fall dead from one whiff of the pickle factory and other similar factories in other countries.' Scramble him like an egg before he hatches. *What is this*? His hand is one of the unbearable mysteries, and the other players can't see his cards, as he rakes in the chips and then says the chips are his cards, a billion on the board.

The Fall of Art

Some years ago in London, I asked Jasper Johns what painting was all about — what are painters really doing? He countered with another question: what is writing about? I did not have an answer then; I have an answer now: The purpose of writing is to make it happen.

What we call 'art' — painting, sculpture, writing, dance, music — is magical in origin. That is, it was originally employed for ceremonial purposes to produce very definite effects. In the world of magic nothing happens unless someone wants it to happen, *wills* it to happen, and there are certain magical formulae to channel and direct the will. The artist is trying to make something happen in the mind of the viewer or reader. In the days of cows-in-the-grass painting, the answer to 'What is the purpose of such painting?' was very simple: to make what is depicted happen in the mind of the viewer; to make him smell the cows and the grass, hear the whistling rustic. The influence of art is no less potent for being indirect. We can leave riots, fires, and wrecks to the journalists. The influence of art has a long-range cultural effect. Jack Kerouac, Allen Ginsberg, Gregory Corso — the Beats wrote a world-wide cultural revolution. Remember that four-letter words could not appear on a printed page twenty-nine years ago. Now, with the breakdown of censorship and the freeing of the Word, the *New York Times* has to print four-letter words used by the President of the United States.

We can trace the tremendous indirect effect of the written word; what about the indirect effect of painting? I have explained how in 1959 Brion Gysin said that writing is fifty years behind painting and applied the montage technique to writing — a technique which had been used in painting for fifty years. As you know, painters had the whole representational position knocked out from under them by photography, and there was in fact a photography exhibition around the turn of the century entitled 'Photography — The Death of Painting'. Premature, but painting did have to get a new look. So painters turned first to montage.

Now the montage is actually much closer to the facts of perception, than representational painting. Take a walk down a city street and put what you have just seen down on canvas. You have seen half a person cut in two by a car, bits and pieces of street signs and advertisements, reflections from shop windows — a montage of fragments. And the same thing happens with words. Remember that the written word is an image. Brion Gysin's cut-up method consists of cutting up pages of text and re-arranging them in montage combinations. Representational painting is dead, unless perhaps the new photo-realism takes hold. Nobody paints cows in the grass any more. Montage is an old device in painting. But if you apply the montage method to writing, you are accused by the critics of promulgating a cult of unintelligibility. Writing is still confined in the sequential representational straitjacket of the novel, a form as arbitrary as the sonnet and as far removed from the actual facts of human perception and consciousness as that fifteenth-century poetical form. Consciousness *is* a cut-up; life is a cut-up. Every time you walk down the street or look out the window, your stream of consciousness is cut by random factors.

Painting in the past hundred years has come from an exclusively representational position, where any number of artists could cover the same material to such a state of fragmentation that every artist must now have his own special point on which there is only room for one artist. Any number of artists can paint country landscapes, but there is only room for one Warhol soup can. It's every artist his own movement now. Here is a question for all schools: If art has undergone such drastic alteration in the past hundred years, what do you think artists will be doing in fifty or a hundred years from now? Of course we can foresee expansion into the realm of exploding art ... A self-destroying TV set, refrigerator, washing-machine, and electric stove going off, leaving a shambles of a gleaming modern apartment; the housewife's dream goes up behind a barrier of shatterproof glass to shield the spectators.

Now here's another angle for you young art hustlers: There is an explosive known as ammonium iodide made by pouring ammonia over iodide crystals or mixing it with tincture for brush work. This compound when it dries is so sensitive that a fly will explode it. I remember how I used to while away the long 1920's afternoons with sugar sprinkled around little heaps of ammonium iodide waiting for the flies to explode in little puffs of purple vapor. So you paint your canvas with ammonium iodide and syrup and release a swarm of flies in the gallery . . . or the people walking around set it off with their vibrations . . . or a team of choir boys touches it off with pop guns . . .

And metal sodium explodes violently on contact with water; so you paint in sodium (which has a beautiful sheen like the side of a silver fish in clear water), and stand well back, and shoot it with a water rifle, or induce a spitting cobra to spit on it and get blown apart. Can sacrificial art be far behind? Cut a chicken's head off and paint with the gushing blood. Disembowel a sheep and paint with its intestines. Or you can do a combo with the sodium number.

Then there will be the famous Mad Bear Floyd, a billionaire painter who covered a twenty-foot montage of porno pictures with thousand-dollar bills soaked in ammonium iodide . . . the montage was laid in the middle of the gallery, then a hamper of thousand-dollar bills rained down and set off the charge, burning a million dollars out of circulation while his agent sold the burnt canvas for $10 million on the spot.

Could this proliferation of competitive angles precipitate a revival of old-time potlatches? The potlatch was a competitive destruction of property carried out until one contestant was ruined and frequently died of shame on the spot. It is interesting to consider American tycoons sitting on this game — blowing up their factories and mines and oil wells, burning their crops and sloshing oil on their beaches, irradiating their land, irrigating with salt water, letting the frozen food rot, burning Rolls-Royces and Bentleys, original Rembrandts, destroying Greek statues with air hammers . . . the American team drops atom bombs on America while China and Russia match us bomb for bomb on their own ground.

The potlatch was invented by the Northwest Coast Indians in the area that is now British Columbia, and it occupied most of their time. Objects destroyed at these uncomfortable occasions included salmon oil, blankets, and coppers. Salmon oil poured on an open fire at the center of the room frequently singed honored guests in the front row, who were obliged by protocol to evince no signs of displeasure. The coppers were engraved shields of thin copper about three feet by two feet, and are now highly valued as curios.

A copper receives its value from the number of potlatches it has weathered: 'THIS IS THE GREAT COPPER BEFORE WHICH OTHER COPPERS PISS THEMSELVES LIKE

BITCH DOGS.' And cowardly coppers shrink back, losing value. You see, a potent copper like this represents so many value units, just as modern art objects may derive value from a series of competitive manipulations: this soup can represents fifty burnt kitchen chairs, twenty urinals, and a Wyeth pig. Competitive over-inflation of values could lead to *La Chute de l'Art*; a total collapse of the art market. Imagine the artist *Bourse* where all the painters stand by their pictures — frenzied phone calls from broker to collector . . . 'Your margin's wiped out, B.J. You gotta cover with the gilt-edge stuff — you know what I mean: Monets, Renoirs, Rembrandts, Picassos . . .' And then: PICASSO SLUMPS SHARPLY AS HIS ENTIRE OUTPUT IS DUMPED ON THE MARKET BY FRANTIC DEALERS . . . As an artist falls off the Board he is obligated by the Board of Health to surrender his pictures to the public incinerator. What art and what artists would survive the holocaust? And how's this for an angle, B.J.? Now this ART grabs you by the balls, see? It hits you in the stomach and dampens your eyes. So the artist gets behind his picture like Punch and Judy and reaches right out through it and grabs a critic by his lapels or slugs him in the guts and sprays him with tear gas. Lots of ways you can slant this. Dead cows in the grass. Dogs leap out of a picture. Vernissage guests savagely clubbed by picture cops. It finally gets so that pictures of dangerous animals, electric chairs, riots, fires, and explosions have the gallery to themselves. Will cows in the grass make a comeback? A critic was gored yesterday. Another drowned in a Monet river and a Bacon exhibition has given rise to unfavorable mutations . . .

What has happened here? Art has become literal and returned to its magical function of making it happen, after a long exile in the realms of imagination where its appetite for happenings has become inordinate. Now suddenly art makes its lethal eruption into the so-called real world. Writing and painting were in the beginning and the word was written image. Now painters paint a future before it is written, having outstripped the retarded twin, writing, and left it back there with the ABC's. Will writing catch up?

A writer who writes a book about a virgin soil epidemic, impregnating his pages with the virus described . . . this book about Poland in a typhus epidemic has typhus lice concealed in the bindings, to be released as book-of-the-month-club ladies turn the pages. Mektoub. It is written. Others have radioactive pages dusted lightly with botulism. The reader is no longer safely reading about sharks while she belches out chocolate fumes; on the page is a powerful shark attractant. Others scorn such crude tricks and rely on the powers of magic — potent spells and curses, often firmed by human sacrifice, flutter from these pestilent pages.

'Beauty kills. Beauty is the murderer,' in the words of Gregory Corso, and painting is reunited with its stupid brother, writing, in books done entirely in pictographs. And by now all books are scented with the appropriate odors and readers are provided with scent bottles for renewal . . . Musky Ozone, Rain on Horseflesh, Empty Locker Rooms . . . Finally comes the Master of the Empty Page, which can only be by initiates

LA CHUTE DU MOT . . . what survives the literalization of art is the timeless ever-changing world of magic caught in the painter's brush, or the writer's words, bits of vivid and vanishing detail. In space any number of painters can dance on the end of a brush, and the writer makes a soundless bow and disappears into the alphabet.

Hemingway

In writing the old-style novel, there was a more or less clear-cut technology and aim. It had a beginning, a middle, and an end. It had plot, it had chapters that maintained suspense, one chapter ending with a suspense situation which led to another chapter on a different character, then back to the suspense situation, building to a climax. The aim was basically to entertain the readers and to sell books. Critics still criticize authors for not writing novels of this sort, even when the novelist is not attempting to do so. Now painting and writing are split into schools and movements. The technology and aim of one movement may be quite different from those of another — if you are doing mobiles, the silkscreen technology of Pop Art is of no use.

Now consider some writers who have said something about the technology of writing. Other writers may not say anything directly, but their concepts of aim and technology may be implicit in the work that is done. I have previously mentioned Graham Greene; he is frankly horrified at the thought of formulating a technology of writing. 'Evelyn Waugh was my very good friend, but we never discussed *writing*.' This is the English game, of course; talk about the weather, talk about anything so long as it isn't important. Not much help from Mr Greene — go to Downside, become a bad Catholic and talk about the weather. He definitely does represent the Gatsby point of view.

There are some do's and don'ts. The sound of the first sentence often determines if anyone will read the book or not. Here's a really atrocious first sentence: 'Herr that unpronounceable name, Hereditary Commander and Chief of the Fleet of Droco, Fisher of the Western Seas, leader in sacrifice, an oracle of the stars, spread his wings and brought them together again in an astonishing thunderclap'. First of all, he has an incomprehensible if not unpronounceable name, he has too many titles, and he already has wings. It's all right if he has wings, but you've got to lead up to it.

Now to quote another first sentence, this time one that makes it: 'Jon Ominar,' (easy to pronounce) 'Emperor of the East', (only got one title) 'reclined in his garden, watching a man being prepared for slow impalement.'

Hemingway has quite a lot to say about writing. He started writing of course as a journalist, which he considered very valuable training. He says use short words and short sentences, although he doesn't always do this by any means. He uses short words, but in very long sentences sometimes. He said to look at the person or object in front of you and transcribe what you see. He also developed a number of exercises, like describing a scene from a viewpoint, then removing the viewpoint and leaving the description. It's as if I described everyone in my class from this viewpoint, then removed myself and just left the description. Take out the 'I'. What his technology boils down to, however, is how to write Hemingway.

The same thing is true of Kerouac and Wolfe. Kerouac had the idea that the first draft was always the best. You should just let the mind flow and type away, and never change it. Well, that's all right for him, but it's not my way of writing. I told him that. I revise. It's how to write Kerouac. And Wolfe is much the same.

Hemingway has been admired and praised by critics for things that he did not do. *The Sun Also Rises* has been acclaimed as the definitive statement of the Lost Generation. It wasn't. There's more of the 1920's in one page of Fitzgerald than in the whole of Hemingway. That wasn't what Hemingway was doing, and he can't be criticized for that. He wasn't evoking a period the way Fitzgerald was.

Hemingway has been described as a master of dialogue. He isn't. No one talks like people talk in Hemingway's novels except people in Hemingway's novels. John O'Hara, not nearly as good a writer, is much more a master of dialogue than Hemingway. You know when you read John O'Hara that that's something he actually heard someone say.

Perhaps it's unfair to say that there's nothing in Hemingway except Hemingway, but that's really the way I feel about it. It's not exactly a criticism, because that's what Hemingway was doing. Hemingway had such a distinctive style that he was trapped in it forever. Nevertheless I think Hemingway came closer to writing himself in present time, closer to writing his life and death, than any other writer. Of course Mishima wrote about *hara kiri* and then later committed it. A French writer of detective stories wrote 'Then he walked across the room, opened the window, and jumped out.' After typing these lines, he walked across the room, opened the window, and jumped out. Well, that's cheating. I mean, Hemingway wrote his death as a character, not as an actor. The difference being, anybody can write 'And then he shot himself' and then shoot himself, if he is prepared to do this. I'm talking about someone who writes 'And then he was shot' and is himself shot by someone else. That's the trick.

All his life Hemingway was plagued by strange incidents. A skylight fell on him in Paris, he broke his toe kicking a gate in, he gaffed a shark and while shooting it in the head with his Colt Woodsman .22, with which he could unerringly shatter wine bottles at 100 feet, the gaff broke and he shot himself in both legs. A lady hunter nearly blew his head off with a shotgun. Several auto accidents; concussion after concussion. The *picadors* are at work.

Hemingway could smell death. He suddenly left a chateau which he said had the stink of death about it, and after he left, the chateau was bombed and several people killed. And he could smell death on others. I have already related incidents.

Hemingway wrote himself as a character. He wrote his life and death so closely that he had to be stopped before he found out what he was doing and wrote about that. There is the moment when the bull looks speculatively from the cape to the matador. The bull is learning. The matador must kill him quick. Two plane crashes in a row, both near Kilimanjaro. The matador has to smash his head against the window of a burning plane. Otherwise he would have found out why two planes crashed near Kilimanjaro; he wrote it. He wrote it in *The Snows of Kilimanjaro*, where Death is the pilot. 'He was pointing now, white white white as far as the eye can see ahead, the snows of Kilimanjaro.' That's the last line.

He who writes death as the pilot of a small plane in Africa should beware of small planes in Africa, especially in the vicinity of Kilimanjaro. But it was written, and he stepped right into his own writing. The brain damage he sustained butting his way out of the burning plane led to a hopeless depression and eventually to his suicide. He put both barrels of a 12 gauge shotgun, No. 6 heavy duck load, against his forehead and tripped both triggers. Fix yourself on that: 'White white white as far as the eye can see ahead . . . the snows of Kilimanjaro.'

68

And unlike the French detective writer, Hemingway wasn't cheating by the act of suicide. He was dead already.

Now suppose you had all the works of a particular writer and could only take some with you, which would be the first you'd throw away? I would get rid of No Man is an Island, *Across the River and into the Trees*, *The Green Hills of Africa*, and *Death in the Afternoon*. In *Across the River* etc. he was writing himself close, but it was not good — not good at all. It is just about the worst of Hemingway's books.

But I would certainly keep *The Snows of Kilimanjaro*, which remains one of the greatest stories about death ever written, because he wrote his own death in that story. Perhaps he was too much of an egoist to write anything else.

Hemingway talks about looking at what is in front of you. Well, a young man who wanted to learn how to write went fishing with Papa Hemingway and asked him about writing. Papa replied, 'Try to figure out why I cussed you out ten minutes ago and how the sun looked on the side of that marlin I just caught.' But between Hemingway's eyes and the object, falls the shadow of Hemingway.

Korzybski says the creative process takes place when you look at an object or a process in silence. And this I think is especially true of dialogue. If you can look at a character without talking, from inner silence, then your character will talk, and you get realistic dialogue. Take something that you actually heard someone say, then let him say that and look at him; pretty soon he'll say some more in the same lines. I remember this amazing used car salesman, from Houston. He was the one who told me 'You know all a Jew wants to do is doddle a Christian girl, you know that yourself.' Well, I didn't say anything, but if I sat him down right here, he could say a lot more along the same lines, I'm sure.

But Hemingway didn't give his characters a chance to talk. He always talked for them, and they all talk Hemingway. Take *The Killers*; it reads well, a good story, and very carefully assembled. The dialogue sounds good, but how good is it? Here are the two killers waiting around for the Swede, gassing meantime with the counterman in this diner.

'What do they do in this town?'

'They eat the dinner. They all come here and eat the big dinner.'

'That's right' says the counterman.

'He says that's right.'

And then they're leaving, they're deciding whether they're going to kill the counterman or not.

'What about sonny boy?'

'He's all right.'

'You've got a lot of luck. You should play the races.'

Of course, these last lines are purely Hemingway. And someone, maybe the counterman, says about the Swede: 'He's cowering in his room.' Also: 'I can't bear to think of him just laying there, knowing he's going to get it.'

'Well you'd better not think of it then.' It's stylized. The killers never really get off the page, you can't really see them. They don't come across with any real menace to the reader.

The Great Gatsby

I would never think seriously about making a film on the Great Gatsby, but it would be an interesting exercise since the film has been made, to decide how one would make it, how it could be made, and if it could be made. And I think the answer is probably not. The picture can be made but I don't think it would be any good. You learn more by considering a difficult book to film, looking at what can and cannot be adapted to the film media, rather than a book written as a film script like JAWS by Peter Benchley, about the great white shark.

Now look at Gatsby, you take the prose away and what is left. Wooden dialogue, creepy action and as for the reconstruction of the 20's you can do that better with a selection of old stock footage. It would be a much better reconstruction of the 20's than in the present film, which I haven't seen yet, in all probability.

The point is, that just asking yourself, how could this book be filmed will lead you to take a closer look at the book and a closer look at Gatsby. As Wolfshine says, 'I saw right away, he was a fine appearing gentlemanly young man. And when he told me he was Oxford, I knew I could use him good.' In stolen bonds you want someone who looks good, but people aren't paid the kind of money Gatsby was making just to look good. In those days $200 a week could buy someone to look good. Young Oxfords like Gatsby, of course this is on the level old sport. Or old dignified good lookers to sit around the front office and Myer Wolfshine was not a man to put out money for nothing, or to put out any more money than he had to for anything. The answer is then, not only was Gatsby in shady and illegal business, he was also very good at covering it up. Stupid people can get rich in a legitimate business just by being there at the right time. I've seen this happen. But no dummy splits the take with Myer Wolfshine, the man who fixed the World Series. And yet, there is scarcely any indication of intelligence in anything that Gatsby says in this book. Occasionally, an indescribable but familiar look on his face indicates that the

Gatsby playing in Wolfshine's league is there. But this whole side of Gatsby is not even hinted at, something reasonably acute is when Caraway says about Daisy, 'her voice is full of money.' Ride on. Don't take the boy for dumber than he is. He couldn't have been dumb at all. Then why does he act so dumb. All this old sport and Oxford routine and lies about his past, tiger hunting and all that bullshit. Buying a big house and filling it with mooching drunks to impress Daisy. Did he have other more accessible girls. Well, we never see them. And why Daisy? Plenty of nice girls falling all over themselves to marry that kind of bread.

In fact, the more closely you look at Gatsby, the more mysterious he becomes. Was he actually psychotic, a split personality, one hand not knowing what the other hand was doing. It doesn't seem likely. You need both hands to function in Wolfshine's area. Were these emotions and this improbable dream skillfully grafted on to him by the author — is that the real secret. That he was a hybrid, a synthetic being, literally created by Fitzgerald's prose, who could not possibly have existed in any other medium. Every now and then that indescribable but familar look comes over his face and he says, 'Pardon me, old sport' and nips into his palatial bathroom, sunken bathtub in pink marble, gold faucets and all the trimmings. And there on the mirror written in silver letters is a passage of what he needs, pure F. Scott prose. He's thin, he can't see his face in the mirror at this point, he reaches under the washstand for his works — antique silver tablespoons, syringe and spike — and the prose drains into the spoon. He draws up a horse syringe full and shoots it in the main line. Now he can see himself. He smooths his hair and straightens his exclusive silken tie and comes out old sporty, a fine appearing Oxford. Well, the wind-up is of course that he runs out of prose, shoots the whole book up and that look is getting more and more familiar. Very much the Jekyll and Hyde theme I think.

He swindles Tom out of all his money, Daisy divorces him under the circumstances to keep her voice full of money and marries Gatsby. Now we're five years later. She's taken to drink, always nipping at a bottle around the house. Gatsby isn't such a gentleman anymore. There he is slapping her around with a wet towel, he has some business connections coming to dinner. But he isn't the kind of man you'd like to take home to introduce to your mother and sister anymore. Hardly the kind of man you'd want to be in the same room with anymore.

Indescribable old sport. Besides he is getting greedy. Wolfshine rather reluctantly puts through a phone call to Chicago and they get him in the swimming pool.

Well take a look at that take, Gatsby on a pneumatic mattress, floating around the pool, tracing a thin red circle in the water. How about that. What was he shot with, a 22 short? It didn't go through and sink the mattress out from under him. Well, in short I think Gatsby is best left alone.

Cut-up from THE GREAT GATSBY and some other sources

It was an extraordinary gift for hope not likely I will ever find again — what dock? The wind had blown off his dreams. Described the fallout as eating the trees. An ashen figure to this blue lawn. And his dream was standing by the swimming pool. Inessential houses began to melt away human dreams the quiet lights in grass outside . . . darkness blew through the room pale flags like ashen trees twisting and then rippled a transitory moment face shadow. What I had almost remembered old unknown world Gatsby borne back into the past. The green light at the end of romantic readiness loud night wings foul dust floating in the wake of negligible fallout. A fragment of lost words frosted wisp of startled air. A breeze blew through the room blew curtains in at one end and out the other like pale flags at the end of Daisy's dock. Lips parted a wisp of startled air a small gust of wind the touch of a cluster of leaves revolved its slowly tracing, like the leg of transit, a thin red circle in the water. Paid a high price for living too long with a single dream. He must have looked up at an unfamiliar sky through frightening leaves and shivered as he found how raw the sunlight was on the scarcely created grass, a new world material without being real, where poor ghosts, breathing dreams like air, drifted about like that ashen figure gliding towards him through the Old Metropole filled with faces dead and gone so he waited listening for a moment to a tuning fork struck upon a star one autumn night five years before they had been walking down a street when the leaves were falling and they came to a place where there were no trees and the sidewalk was white with moonlight already crumbling through the powdery air. But above the gray land and the spasms of bleak dust you perceive the eyes of Doctor T.J. Eckleburg blue and gigantic looking out from a pair of enormous yellow spectacles brooding over the solemn dumping ground.

The Johnson Family

I first heard this expression in a book called *You Can't Win* by Jack Black, the life story of a burglar. The book was published in 1924 and I read it as a boy fascinated by this dark furtive purposeful world. I managed to get a copy and re-read the book with poignant nostalgia. Between the reader in 1924 and the reader in 1980 falls the shadow of August 6, 1945, one of the most portentous dates of history.

Train whistles across a distant sky. This is a peep show back to the world of rod-riding yeggs and peat men and cat burglars, bindle stiffs, gay cats and hobo jungles and Salt Chunk Mary the fence in her two storey red brick house down by the tracks somewhere in Idaho. She keeps a blue porcelain coffee pot and an iron pot of pork and beans always in the fire. You eat first and talk business later the watches and rings sloped out on the kitchen table by the chipped coffee mugs. She named a price and she didn't name another. Mary could say no quicker than any woman I ever knew and none of them ever meant yes. She kept the money in a cookie jar but nobody thought about that. Her cold gray eyes would have seen the thought and maybe something goes wrong on the next lay. John Law just happens by or a citizen comes up with a load of 00 buck shot into your soft and tenders.

In this world of shabby rooming houses, furtive gray figures in dark suits, hop joints and chili parlors the Johnson Family took shape as a code of conduct. To say someone is a Johnson means he keeps his word and honors his obligations. He's a good man to do business with and a good man to have on your team. He is not a malicious, snooping, interfering self-righteous trouble making person.

You get to know a Johnson when you see one and you get to know those of another persuasion. I remember in the Merchant Marine training center at Sheepshead Bay when the war ended. Most of the trainees quit right then and there was a long line to turn in equipment which had to be checked out item by item; some of us had only been there a few days and we had no

74

equipment to turn in. So we hoped to avoid standing for hours, days perhaps in line for no purpose. I remember this spade cat said, 'Well, we're going to meet a nice guy or we're going to meet a prick.' We met a prick but we managed to find a Johnson.

Yes you get to know a Johnson when you see one. The cop who gave me a joint to smoke in the wagon. The hotel clerk who tipped me off I was hot. And sometimes you don't see the Johnson. I remember a friend of mine asked someone to send him a cake of hash from France. Well the asshole put it into a cheap envelope with no wrapping and it cut through the envelope. But some Johnson had put it back in and sealed the envelope with tape.

Years ago I was stranded in the wilds of East Texas and Bill Gains was sending me a little Pantapon through the mail and he invented this clever code and telegrams are flying back and forth.

'Urgently need pants.'

'Panic among dealers. No pants available.'

This was during the war in a town of 200 people. By rights we should have had the FBI swarming all over us. I remember the telegraph operator in his office in the railroad station. He had a kind, unhappy face. I suspect he was having trouble with his wife. Never a question or comment. He just didn't care what pants stood for. He was a Johnson.

A Johnson minds his own business. But he will help when help is needed. He doesn't stand by while someone is drowning or trapped in a wrecked car. Kells Elvins, a friend of mine, was doing 90 in his Town and Country Chrysler on the way from Pharr, Texas to Laredo. He comes up over a rise and there is a fucking cow right in the middle of the road on the bridge. He slams on the brakes and hits the cow doing 60. The car flips over and he is pinned under it with a broken collar bone covered from head to foot with blood and guts and cowshit. So along comes a car with some salesmen in it. They get out cautiously. He tells them just how to jack the car up and get it off him but when they see that *blood* they don't want to know. They don't want to get mixed up with anything like that. They get back in their car and drive away. Then a truck driver comes along. He doesn't need to be told exactly what to do, gets the car off Kells and takes him to a hospital. The truck driver was a Johnson. The salesmen were shits like most salesmen. Selling shit and they are shit.

The Johnson family formulates a Manichean position where

good and evil are in conflict and the outcome is at this point uncertain. It is *not* an eternal conflict since one or the other must win a final victory.

Which side are you on?

I recollect Brion Gysin, Ian Sommerville and your reporter were drinking an espresso on the terrace of a little café on the Calle de Vigne in Tangier . . . after lunch a dead empty space . . . Then this Spaniard walks by. He is about 50 or older, shabby, obviously very poor carrying something wrapped in brown paper. And our mouths fell open as we exclaimed in unison

'My God that's a harmless looking person!'

He passed and I never saw him again, his passing portentous as a comet reminding us how rare it is to see a harmless looking person, a man who minds his own business and gets along as best he can in a world largely populated by people of a very different persuasion, kept alive by the hope of harming someone, on their way to the Comisario to denounce a neighbor or a business rival leaving squiggles and mutterings of malevolence in their wake like ugly little spirits.

He passed and I never saw him again. But I recognized him. He was a Johnson. You get to know a Johnson when you see one . . . the cop in New Orleans who slipped me a joint to smoke in the paddy wagon, the doctor who gave me a shot of morphine in the hospital while a colleague was muttering about the moral questions involved, the hotel clerk who tipped me the law is on its way, better move out fast.

February 3, 1982 . . . A program on El Salvador . . . a reporter has contacted a guerrilla group. One look at those faces and I know where I stand. I know them all. They are Johnsons. The reporter is checking the contention of the junta and the Reagan administration that the guerrillas are armed with Soviet weapons via Cuba and Nicaragua . . .

'Let's see your guns.'

Young man has a Belgian assault rifle 9M . . . handsome boy about 20 has an M-16, a little fat boy about 16 has a .22 held together with wire and tape.

'Fifty years old' he tells us, smiling.

Man in his thirties, nice smile: 'Me, I got no gun.'

Well where are the Russian K-47s you are supposed to be getting from Cuba?'

'No hay.' (There aren't any)

Look at these faces. Nice faces. Johnson faces. You can't

fake it. That old Spaniard couldn't have been a KGB Colonel, or a Cousin, or M-16. No agent could have that cover. Because it isn't a cover. It's the real thing.

Three guns for 20 men. Shy handsome boy of 15 has been with the guerrillas since he was 14. Why? No ideology no rubbish. Self defence. Once you take up arms against a bunch of shits there is no way back. Lay down your arms and they will kill you. I've seen the Policía Nacionale in action in Colombia during the civil war. Vicious thugs. No Johnson faces there.

That's all the orientation I need to make up my mind about El Salvador. Don't want to hear Haig's lies or any other lies. Haig is no Johnson. He's got one of the most basically dishonest faces I ever saw. And the same look on his face when he lies as General Westmoreland . . . LIE LIE LIE written all over it.

Civilian Defence

C.D. *Civilian Defence* started with names on cards. These ID cards identify the bearer — photo and fingerprints, description and address — as a Civil Defence Agent. Each card has a number. I think it was no accident that one of the original 13 early card holders was a computer programmer. The idea behind the C.D. card was and is very simple: We will follow the example set by the Guardian Angels. We will patrol the subways, acting to stop crime, to aid and protect victims of crimes in accordance with our plain duty as citizens and fellow humans. We hope that our example will inspire other citizens to help themselves and each other. We hope to instill a get-in-this-and-help reflex, instead of a keep-out-of-it-walk-away-shut-your-lousy-mouth reflex. We intend to make it fashionable to defend ourselves and others. We will be of all ages and all walks of life. You join by filling out a form and obtaining a C.D. Card. You are expected to patrol one night a month but may do so as often as you wish.

The Angels carry no weapons. Our policy on weapons is that the field agent on patrol may carry whatever weapons he wants to carry, for which he assumes the legal responsibility. The most commonly carried legal weapon is a cane or walking stick. He can equip himself at a C.D. store (in the beginning these were simply lost addresses) after showing his C.D. card. At first the stores sold mostly canes of heavy wood and simple designs, with a brochure showing some of the basics of cane fighting. Weapons of doubtful legality were tear gas guns and short sticks carried concealed. It was C.D. policy to try out various weapons for a court decision. This attracted some sharp legal brains.

C.D. caught on like mad. And with it came a new spirit of release. The ordinary citizen felt that he didn't have to take it lying down anymore. He could do something about it right now. Join C.D.

The T.O.T. Decision gave us tremendous impetus. *The Tool of Trade Decision*, which involved a concealed awl and a dead punk, stipulated that a citizen may not be arrested or charged for carrying the tools of his trade unless the artifacts in question are specifically controlled by other statutes. The defendant was a part-time leather worker.

'You can drive a trailer truck through T.O.T.' wailed the Commissioner. 'They'll carry anything and call it a tool of their trade.'

We are setting up centers where courses in stick and hand to hand fighting are given. Friendly C.D. Advisors are there to help you. They will give you a list of reliable merchants who install security devices in apartments. They will put you in touch with other people in your neighborhood who may have the same problems. We advertise on the subways.

Poster shows the grinning Buddies all with C.D. T-shirts, patches, arm bands, hat bands . . .

THERE'S SAFETY IN NUMBERS
BECOME A SUBWAY BUDDY

Get to know the other citizens who ride the same trains
at the same time you do. Become a Subway Buddy.
Every Buddy will help you when you need help, and
you will help every Buddy. JOIN NOW. Take one . . .

Subway Buddies really caught on. I mean, who would slink around *not* being a Subway Buddy? There they are on the platform laughingly comparing their canes and staffs and golf clubs. 'For close in chops I favor a niblick. For the home stretch a loaded driver.' Now they settle in a car and leer knowingly at each other. A plumber fondles a heavy pipe wrench. Nobody's going to chain snatch *his* subway buddies. The C.D. Stores are now vast weapon supermarkets. Here is a fetching array of carpenter suits in leather and denim with reinforced pockets and pouches and sheaths for awls and ice picks, do fridge jobs on the side you know, and those lovely ice hammer crow bars, all one gorgeous hunka stainless . . . and exquisite ball pens with whip handles.

'Don't forget your Union Card, sir. You are now a member of the C.D. Carpenter's Union.' The clerk winks broadly. 'It's legal as Hell. And this battery powered drill right in his muggin' eye sir! And this air hammer can be used as a walking stick. It's a rupturin' perforating tool, if you'll pardon the expression, sir.' We stroll on to the Exterminator section. 'Now this blower shoots a finely divided black cyanide dust. One good whiff sir. Not recommended for *crowd* situations sir.'

The Farmer's Market gets a big play. Window Box Farmers

fancy themselves as Death with a scythe, and one old joker incinerated two rowdies with a flame thrower.

'Farmer you know. We use them for killing weeds. Never withou: it . . . haw haw . . .'

Some of these devices were shot down in the courts. Flame throwers and all incendiary devices, for example, were outlawed by Fire Department regulations, but new ones kept popping up until the courts were jammed with weapons cases.

'Darling I've been doing a lot of research and there is absolutely no license required to buy a flint lock or percussion gun, or to carry one. Or a sword for that matter, carried openly.'

'My God!' screamed the old transit cop. 'Fifty of them with cavalry sabres and civil war revolvers.'

And the Golfers with their loaded drivers and their charge cry: 'FORE!' The Baseball Players, brutal burly men, beat your muggin' brains out. The Polo Boys, lithe aloof young men faultlessly attired in riding clothes. They are adept at tripping with their mallets, or they may prefer to disembowel a mugger with a back kick of razor sharp spurs, bare their teeth and roll their eyes like a fucking horse as they emit their terrible whinny of triumph.

C.D. becomes obligatory like jury duty. We computerize our records. We have records not only on those who have committed crimes, but on those who can be expected to commit certain types of crimes in the future. These assessments are based on field agents' reports. A Field Agent knows everybody in his district inside out. He records their voices. He takes pictures. A lot of this goes into the *Top Secret Only Fools* file. (Only fools do those villains pity who are punished e're they have done their mischief.)

There is no stopping C.D. Knock on any door. Walk down any street. C.D. T-shirts, patches, arm bands, rings, discreet gold lapel pins, luminous rainbow hat bands — 'Her glow in the dark.' Many wear their C.D. card in a little plastic window. C.D.! C.D.! C.D.! Our deadly field hands, as we jokingly call them, are everywhere stopping crime. They know where to look they know who to follow.

'They are undermining the very concept of police!' the Commissioner moans.

'We are the police and we need no criminals,' was the terse telex rejoinder from Wise Guy the C.D. Computer.

Any C.D. member can put this solution to any question into Wise Guy, who chews them all up and spits out a solution. Wise

Guy thinks that some crimes are much more portentous, that is more basically *criminal*, than others. These crimes receive special attention.

Is it good for our space program? This basic criterion is programmed into Wise Guy and he dictates his decisions. Man just released from mental hospital stabs a *sleeping* man to death with a sharp stick; little bitch sees someone *sleeping* on the subway, dowses his hair with lighter fluid and sets him afire. 'I just felt like it,' she said. Other victims have been old transients *sleeping* on pavements or in vacant lots. The common denominator is *sleeping*.

On space craft people may have to go into bio-stasis. We need some little whore prowling around turning off our life support systems? Now human beings are merely the carriers for certain entities. We don't want any carriers of this entity in our surroundings. So we organized a crack team of outraged citizens and grabbed a torcher dowsed it with water and threw it on the third rail. Gave that entity pause. And here is another. It happens every Halloween: Little girl three years old been trick-or-treatin' comes back and her mother finds a pin in a pink sugar candy with cream centers, the pinhead white to look like sugar. Now this can only be described as poisoning the water supply. We don't want anything like that aboard space ship earth.

The Colonel looked into the fire. He is a member of the elite corps of E.S. — *Evolutionary Security*. The function of E.S. is to create a safe environment for biologic experiments free from brutish, malignant interference.

'Of course we knew it would come to this sooner or later — individual assassinations. 'Hits' you call them I believe. Well it wasn't too hard to find this one. Little frame house reeked of it. Not even a weed will grow in the yard. She works in the library, which is almost never used because no one can get the book he orders, and if he does, keeps getting nasty letters for years demanding the return of books he never withdrew. She used sleeping pills. It was easy. We also impounded some interesting documents. For years this old witch had been writing letters to newspapers. Some, dating back to the days of capital punishment,* were abusive anonymous letters sent to the parents of those executed, timed to arrive on the day of execution. And here is a four year old boy attacked by guard dogs, critically ill in hospital, and she writes to the mother: 'He should die soon. I hope he will.'

* Capital punishment fell into disuse in the U.S. for some years, but has been restored by the judiciary under President Reagan.

And her diary . . . 'Christmas 1848 . . . I think I've made a "catch".

'December 27 . . . My prayers have been answered.'

She was a very religious woman. The only book in her house was the Bible.

At the very moment of her death waves of happiness and euphoria swept the neighborhood: 'It was a feeling of *relief*,' one neighbor said. 'Like something *awful* went away and you can breathe again.'

'C.D. can stand for *Common Decency*. When someone needs help you give help. When someone wants to be left alone you leave him alone. He has a right to his space. The principles of the Johnson Family.

'God must have loved the Johnsons because he made so many of them.'

We postulate that man is an artifact designed for space travel. He is not designed to remain in his present biologic state any more than a tadpole is designed to remain a tadpole. This postulate, agreed upon, gives us a standard evaluation. Is a proposed course of action conducive to realizing space conditions? Art, science, technology, what is it contributing to the space program? As for individuals, ask yourself — would I like to be *in space* with *that* person? Postulate that there is no privacy and no deceit possible in space: Your innermost thoughts, feelings and intentions are immediately apparent to those around you. So you want to be careful who *is* around you.

And what has prevented the Johnsons from realizing their potential for space travel? Who is keeping us from realizing our biological and spiritual destiny? These people are known as shits. They can't mind their own business, because they have no business of their own to mind any more than a small pox virus. The mark of a basic shit is that he has to be RIGHT. And in order to be RIGHT he has to make someone else WRONG. We know that the shits will take action against us since they are artifacts specifically designed to keep us out of space.

Our research is directed towards effecting biologic alterations in the human artifact. The human body is much too dense for space conditions. However, we have a model to hand that is much less dense in fact almost weightless: the astral or dream body. This lighter body, a 'body of light,' as Crowley called it, is much more suited to space conditions.

Recent experiments have shown that dreaming is a biological

necessity like sleep. The dream serves as a link to our destiny in space. Deprived of that air line we die. And when we see the Rev. Jerry Falwell and his Moral Majority cutting our airlines, we classify such behaviour as criminal interference.

The step into space is a step into the unknown, a change as drastic as the transition from water to land. Those who now attempt to impose by sheer force a rigid dogma can only be seen as the mortal enemies of C.D. They threaten the life and the space destiny of every decent well-intentioned Johnson. It is the role of C.D. to protect new life forms in the vulnerable stages of mutation. Perhaps many times before beautiful new life forms with great potentials were brutishly stamped out by those who cannot tolerate anything different from their stupid, bigoted, hideous selves. This is a Manichean conflict. The outcome is in doubt.

Sexual Conditioning

The whole area of sex is still shrouded in mystery and ignorance. Any attempt to apply objective experimental methods to the study of sexual phenomena has been firmly discouraged. People who do not think of themselves as religious — doctors, sociologists, psychiatrists — are still thinking in terms laid down by the Christian Church. The church assumes that any sexual activity except intercourse with a legal spouse is absolutely wrong because the Bible says so. They condemn so-called deviant behavior in the strongest terms. Psychiatrists, substituting the word 'sick' for 'wrong', follow the old Christian line. Recent experiments with electric brain stimulation, however, has provided a much more precise means of conditioning than psychoanalysis and psychotherapy.

Admittedly, a homosexual can be conditioned to react sexually to a woman, or to an old boot for that matter. In fact, both homo- and heterosexual experimental subjects *have* been conditioned to react sexually to an old boot, and you can save a lot of money that way.

In the same way, heterosexual males can be conditioned to react sexually to other men. Who is to say that one is more desirable than the other? Who is competent to lay down sexual dogmas and impose them on others? The latter-day apologists of St. Paul who call themselves psychiatrists have little to recommend them but their bad statistics. They couldn't get away with statistics like that in any other line of business. Suppose you run a business and the traffic department isn't getting the consignments out. They say they need more money and more personnel, and the situation gets worse. Consignments stack up like patients in a state hospital. They say they need yet more money and more personnel to cope with the ever-growing traffic problem. How long before you fire the entire traffic department and get someone in there who can do the job? Psychiatrists say they need more money and personnel to deal with the ever-growing problem of mental illness, and the more money and personnel that is channelled into this bottomless pit, the higher the statistics on mental illness climb. Personally I think that mental illness is largely a psychiatric invention.

On December 3rd, 1973, the American Psychiatric Association decided that homosexuality would no longer be considered a mental deviation. Well, if they have more mental patients now than they can handle, it would seem to be a step in the right direction to remove homosexuals from this category. But the decision has caused a storm of protest. One psychiatrist compared the decision to 'a psychiatric Watergate which we hope won't be our Waterloo . . .' They just don't like to see any prospective patients escaping; it could start a mass walkout. Doctor Charles Socarides, associate clinical professor of psychiatry at the Albert Einstein Clinic staunchly opposes the new A.P.A. approach: 'The A.P.A. has done what all civilizations have trembled to do . . . tamper with the biologic role between the sexes.' Fancy that — and in a letter to *Playboy* in June of 1970, Dr Socarides says, 'Five hundred million years of evolution have established the male/female standard as *the* functionally healthy pattern of human sexual fulfillment.'

Just a minute here, Doctor — the human species is not more than one million years old according to the earliest human remains so far discovered. Other species have had a longer run. Three hundred million years have established a big mouth that can bite off almost anything and a gut that can digest it, as a functionally healthy pattern for sharks. About 130 million years established large size as functionally healthy for dinosaurs. What may be functionally healthy at one time is not necessarily so under altered conditions, as the bones of discontinued models bear silent witness. But sharks, dinosaurs, and psychiatrists don't want to change.

The sexual revolution is now moving into the electronic stage. Recent experiments in electric brain stimulation indicate that sexual excitement and orgasm can be produced at push-button control or push-button *choice*, depending on who is pushing the buttons. None of these bits of technology are in the future; the knowledge, and most of the hardware, exist today.

For example, there already exists a device that can be used in conjunction with bio-feedback and electric brain stimulation. I quote from an article by Patrick Carr, entitled 'The Sonic Dildo: At Last, the No-Contact Orgasm', about how a man named How Wachspress of San Franscisco has developed an audio machine that puts sound into the human body through the skin: 'He begins to play with the controls of his synthesizer, programming a series of sonic patterns for sensual effect, and this *feeling* begins to spread down from my stomach toward my crotch, most certainly turning me on and relaxing me at the same time. My instant desire is for the same, only *louder*. Lovely sensations spread over my hips, crotch, stomach, and spine, and I am beginning to sense surprisingly precise nuances of tone and pattern as How performs 'frequency sweeps', a sharp attack with a long decay, a long rise with a sharp decay ... oh, *yes* ... "Very Indian, huh?" says How. "Y'know, I'm certain that ragas would be great for the body ..." Afterward, disconnected from the unit, I experienced a wonderful body-buzzing calm.'

In terms of human sexuality what could it mean? Apparently there is no limit. A partner evoked by sophisticated electric brain stimulation could be as real and much more satisfying than the boy or girl next door. The machine can provide you with anything or anybody you want. All the stars in Hollywood living or dead are there for your pleasure. Sated with superstars, you can lay Cleopatra, Helen of Troy, Isis, Madame Pompadour, or Aphrodite. You can get fucked by Pan, Jesus Christ, Apollo or the Devil himself. Anything you like likes you when you press the buttons. Boys, girls, gods, angels, devils. The appropriate sets can also be plugged in. Sex in an Egyptian palace? A Greek glade? A 1910 outhouse? Roman baths? Space capsule? 1920 rumble seat? Pirate ship? Log cabin? Mongol tent? And none of the sweat that goes with log cabins, tents, and pirate ships. It's ready built, waiting for you, and you can leave any time you want.

Could real partners compete? Well, maybe. Experiments in autonomic shaping have demonstrated that subjects can learn to control these responses and reproduce them at will once they learn where the neutral buttons are located. Just decide what you want, and your local sex adjustment center will match your brain waves and provide you with a suitable mate of whatever sex, real or imaginary, while you wait. It is now possible to provide every man and woman with the best sex tricks he or she can tolerate without blowing a fuse. And any candidate running on that ticket should poll a lot of votes and bring a lot of issues right out into the open:

'I promise you that I will disband the Army and the Navy and channel the entire defense budget into setting up sexual adjustment centers throughout the United States. And I promise you further that the psychic energy generated in these

86

centers will turn any and all prospective enemies into friends, into *intimate* friends, as other nations follow our shining example.'

'Control buttons to the People.'

On Freud and the Unconscious

Freud, who was one of the early researchers to point out the heavy toll in mental illness exacted by 19th century materialistic capitalism, never questioned the underlying ethic. He felt that we have paid a high price for what he calls civilization, and the price has been worth it. It did not occur to him to ask if the price was necessary. There is no reason why we could not enjoy the advantages of so called civilization without crippling conflicts. Freud uncovered the extent of marginal, unconscious thinking, but failed to realize that such thinking may be highly useful and advantageous. Where Id and Super Ego was, there shall Ego be, is certainly an outmoded objective. In fact the conscious ego is in many activities a liability as anyone knows who has set out to master a physical skill like shooting, fencing, boxing, driving, flying. Only when your responses become automatic and operative without conscious volition can you perform effectively.

The Buddhists have always regarded the ego as a spiritual hindrance. I recall a heckler who asked Chogyam Trungpa Rinpoche why people stand up when he comes into the room. Trungpa replied 'From respect.' 'Respect for what?' the heckler demanded. 'Egolessness,' his Holiness replied. Buddhism, and a number of other spiritual disciplines, are precisely designed to break down the ego. And I can testify from my own experience that the ego is an artistic liability. The best writing and painting is only accomplished when the ego is superseded or refuted. An artist is in fact transcribing from the unconscious.

Freud's concept of the unconscious derived from his clinical experience. He observed a number of crippling symptoms that he traced to unconscious conflicts. So he tended to regard the unconscious as destructive or at least as a repository of irrational and atavistic urges. How then can a disadvantageous factor existing in the human psyche be explained biologically? Freud says that restraints on unconscious urges are necessary to hold a civilization together, but this explanation is altogether too rational, presupposing a consciously agreed upon social

88

contract to suppress the irrational. He must have seen the flaws in this argument and went on to develop his highly dubious concept of a Death Instinct and a Life Instinct in eternal conflict. Here he is getting close to the Manichean position of postulating a battle between the forces of Good and Evil. Though Freud criticized Jung for aspiring to be a philosopher and prophet rather than a simple clinician, he is certainly open to the same criticism. Ego, Super Ego and Id, floating about in a vacuum without any reference to the human nervous system, strike me as highly dubious metaphysical concepts.

In his later years Freud grudgingly accepted telepathy since he had encountered so many instances of telepathic exchange in his clinical practice.

I recall when I was in analysis with Doctor Federn, a number of telepathic exchanges turned up. For example I saw him in a dream giving out candy to children and told him to be careful or he would get a reputation as a child molester. When I related this dream he told me that he had actually given out candy on a vacation at Cape Cod and then realized, in his own words, 'that people might think it is a sexy old man.' And he told me of an analyst of his acquaintance who had collected twelve hundred instances of telepathy from his practise. But Doctor Federn refused to admit implications of telepathy. When I suggested that the curse of a malignant person might be effective he categorically denied that such a thing was possible. 'Witches,' he said 'are hysterics and their victims are paranoid.' However, if we admit telepathic contact we must logically admit that such contact can be as damaging as face to face contact.

Freud, while admitting the occurrence of telepathy, thought of it as an atavistic and undesirable vestige going back to the protoplasmic antiquity. It did not occur to him that this faculty could be useful or that it is used every day by ordinary people. The most hard-bitten police officer plays his hunches. He *knows* when a suspect is lying. Observe two horse traders and you will see telepathy in action. This one won't go above a certain figure. The other won't come down below a certain figure. You can see the closing figure taking shape in their minds. I will return later to the practical uses of ESP abilities. It is to be remembered that the unconscious was much more unconscious in Freud's day than in ours. Sexual taboos were much more rigid and sexual behaviour was literally un-mentionable. Four letter words could not appear on a printed page and the soft core porn sold now at any newstand would have been unthinkable in the 19th century. Hysteria, the classical example of unconsciously motivated symptoms, was quite common in clinical practice and is, I understand, quite rare at this present time.

So the unconscious is not a stable factor, but varies greatly from one individual to another and from one culture to another. I recall an analyst practising in Morocco who told me that the super ego seemed to be lacking or at least different in his Arab patients. In the west we seem to be at a stage which could be called the semi or marginally conscious. And perhaps we can look forward to a time when the unconscious will merge with the conscious.

Freud thought that the ego, super ego and id must eventually be placed onto a physiological basis and modern brain area. Research is coming close to accomplishing this. Professor Delgado, author of a book entitled *Physical Control of the Mind*, has demonstrated that irrational fear, aggression, anxiety, can be produced by the electrical stimulation of certain brain areas. All the symptoms of unconscious conflict can be turned off and on by the flick of a switch. Biofeedback has demonstrated that such autonomic reactions as sweating, increased heart beat rate and blood pressure, which are symptoms of unconscious conflict, can be brought under conscious control.

I do not think of myself as a materialist but I do insist that anything that effects the human nervous system must have a point of reference that is a definite location in the human nervous system. Julian Jaynes in his book *The Origins of Consciousness in the Breakdown of the Bicameral Mind* puts forward a thesis that would tend to locate the unconscious in the non-dominant brain hemisphere. His theory postulates that the unconscious ego, the Id, is a comparatively recent development that occurred in the period from about 1000 to 800 B.C. Before that man obeyed the Voice of God which emanated from the non-dominant brain hemisphere, without question. There was no questioning entity. They literally had no ego but were governed by what Freud calls the super ego and their instinctual drives, the Id. He bolsters his thesis with ample clinical evidence gleaned from accident cases where part of the brain has been damaged or destroyed, and by experiments involving electrical stimulation of the non-dominant brain hemisphere which causes normal subjects to hear voices. However, the non-dominant hemisphere is not simply a source of irrational symptoms but performs a number of useful and in fact essential services. For example, the simplest spatial problems become extremely difficult to solve if the non-dominant brain hemisphere is damaged.

So Freud's objective, where Id and Super Ego were, there shall Ego be, would be highly damaging if it were achieved. A more viable goal would be to bring about a harmonious coexistence of the two brain hemispheres rather than attempting to gain a precarious territorial advantage for the so-called rational hemisphere.

As soon as Jaynes puts forward his thesis that consciousness as we know it did not exist prior to 1000 B.C., the question of defining consciousness arises. Well definitions are usually not necessary and frequently confusing. We do not need to define electricity, to arrive at any formulation as to what electricity essentially is, to know how electricity operates and to use it effectively. I don't have to define something in order to use it or describe its properties. Common sense formulations will suffice. We don't need to define consciousness in order to map the areas of consciousness and to locate it tentatively in the cerebral cortex, the verbal centers and the dominant brain hemisphere. We can say further that consciousness is that instance that would attempt to define consciousness presenting the paradox of a ruler measuring itself. And we can tentatively locate the unconscious in the back brain and the non-dominant brain hemisphere. And however we derive consciousness it is obvious that certain activities require more of it than others. We need more consciousness crossing a city street than walking down a country lane. Bicameral man didn't need much consciousness. His environment was vastly more uniform and predictable and he was, acording to Jaynes's thesis, getting his orders straight from the voice of God in the non-dominant brain hemisphere. He was all Id and Super Ego with little or no Ego. Introspection was simply impossible.

According to Jaynes the awe in which the priest king was held derived from his ability to produce his voice in the brains of his loyal subjects. To hear on this level is to obey and there is no room for arguments or alternative courses of action. So consciousness, which decides between one course of action and another, had no function. The bicameral mind broke down in a period of social unrest, war, natural disasters and migrations. This period of chaos led to conflicting voices and eventually to the conscious ego as we know it today. A symptom of the bicameral breakdown was the use of oracles and divination. Divination, which puts the seeker in touch with his own consciousness, had no place in the bicameral mind since man was already merged with his unconsciousness. Now he had to go to oracles for the voice of God and the ego, in eternal conflict with itself and with other egos, slowly emerged.

But the voice of God was not dead. People continued to hear and obey voices and they still do. *New York Post*, Friday January 18, 1980: 'Escaped mental patient tells police that voices commanded him to bash in the head of elderly passerby.' Why are the voices obeyed? If bicameral man obeyed the voices willingly and without question, modern man seems compelled to obey *because the voice is there*. The voice has taken over motor centers by its presence. Julian Jaynes cites the case of a man who was ordered by a voice to drown himself. Rescued by a lifeguard the recovered patient gives this account of his experience. 'The deep voices, loud and clear, pounded in as though all parts of me had become ears with my fingers and my legs and my head hearing the words. There is the ocean. Drown yourself. Just walk in and keep walking. *I knew by its cold command I had to obey it.*'

What was the origin of the voices in the first place? Jaynes does not venture to speculate. If we can produce voices by electrical stimulation of the non-dominant brain hemisphere, perhaps the voices were originally produced by electrical stimulation coming from without. We approach the realms of science fiction which is rapidly becoming science fact. Fifteen years ago experiments in Norway indicated that voices can be produced directly in the brain by an electromagnetic field. Progress along these lines is probably classified material.

The difference between a normal and a pathological manifestation is quantitative, a question of degree. When you think of someone you may hear his voice distinctly just as you may see his image. You will observe that some people are more audible than others. I have but to think of a certain English lady of my acquaintance and hear her voice as if she were sitting next to me. Other friends of hers report the same experience. So what is the line between memory and hallucination?

Psychiatrists tend to assume that any voices anyone hears in his head originate there, and that they do not and can not have an extraneous origin. The whole psychiatric dogma that voices are the imaginings of a sick mind has been called in question by voices which are of extraneous origin and are objectively and demonstrably there on tape. Freud says that errors and slips of the tongue are unconsciously motivated. And I agree that errors and accidents are *motivated*. For example dropping or spilling things. It may not be easy to remember what you were thinking about when this happened. In my case it usually happens when I am thinking about someone I dislike or with whom I am quarrelling. It is a demonstration then of hostility but the hostility may be quite unconscious. Other errors may have a more complex etiology and often seem quite inexplicable.

Here is an example. In Boulder, Colorado, I went to a fish market called Pelican Pete's. They accept American Express cards so I proffered what I thought was my American Express card in payment. However, I had accidentally handed him my Chase Manhattan Bank check cashing card. A simple error is it not? Months later I was on my way to cash a check at the Chase Manhattan Bank at Houston and Broadway. Just across from the bank some one had set up a street stand and was selling fish. I noted the fish stand in passing. So when I got in the bank I accidentally handed the teller my American Express card instead of my Chase Manhattan check cashing card. What is unconscious here? Only the moment in which the error is made. But a whole train of association leads up to this moment. One has the impression of another presence muttering away at all hours of the day and night of which one is only partially or occasionally aware. One rule applies: lightning always strikes twice in the same place. One mistake with cards makes another mistake that much more probable. But the motivation remains obscure.

Freud states that dreams always express the fulfillment of a wish. The dream content may be frightening or repugnant to the dreamer because the wish expressed is unconscious. Consider the syndrome of combat nightmares. The veteran dreams he is back in a combat situation. In what sense is this wish fulfillment?

Recent studies of dream and sleep have yielded a wealth of data that was not available in Freud's day. Perhaps the most important discovery is the fact that dreams are a biologic necessity. Deprived of REM sleep, experimental subjects show all the symptoms of sleeplessness, no matter how much dreamless sleep they are allowed. They become irritable and restless and experience hallucinations. No doubt prolonged deprivation would result in death.

An interesting discovery by Jouvet is the fact that all warm blooded animals including birds dream, but cold blooded animals do not dream. He attributes this to the fact that the neural tissue of the cold blooded animals renews itself and heals from traumas whereas the neural tissue of the warm blooded animals, once damaged, does not heal. There is however a part of the mammalian brain that does have the ability to heal and this is the pons. If the pons is removed experimentally from cats they act out their dreams lapping imaginary milk and chasing dream mice. The pons then serves to immobilize the body during dreams. Further, research should shed light on the function of dreams, which is far from being understood.

John Dunne, an English physicist and mathematician, wrote a book called *An Experiment With Time* that was first published in 1924. Dunne wrote his dreams down and observed that they contained material from the future as well as the past. He gives a number of examples and states that anyone who will take the trouble to keep a pad and pencil by his bed and write his dreams as they occur will, after a period of time, turn up precognitive dreams. He observed that if you dream of a future occurrence say a flood or fire or plane crash . . . you are dreaming not about the occurrence itself but of the time that you learn of the occurrence . . . Usually through a newspaper picture. In other words you are dreaming your own future time track. I have written my dreams down over a period of years. And I have noticed that, if I don't write the dream down immediately I will in many cases forget it, no matter how many times I go over the dream in my mind. I wake up, too much trouble to turn on the light but I can't possibly forget it and I do. It would seem the memory traces of dream experience are much fainter than with waking experience. I have experienced a number of precognitive dreams that are often quite trivial and irrelevant. For example I dreamed that a landlady showed me a room with five beds in it and I protested that I didn't want to sleep in a room with five people. Some weeks later I went to a reading in Amsterdam and the hotel keeper did show me a room with five beds in it. Well the sponsor took me to another hotel. In another dream I saw a wardrobe floating by. The next day I was in the Café de France in Tangier and looked up and there was the wardrobe floating by the window. A man was carrying it on his back with a strap around his forehead so I could not see the bearer just the wardrobe. Precognition is not confined to the dream state. In fact I have the impression it is going on all the time. Nor is the dream state confined to sleep. It is my experience that the dream state goes on all the time, and that we can contact it in a waking state. Years ago I was into gambling. I recall I was standing in line at the race track to make a bet and the tune SMILES was playing over and over in my head. But I didn't bet on Smiles the winning horse. Anyone who has done any target shooting or archery will tell you that he knows just before he shoots or looses an arrow whether it will or will not hit the target.

For me dreams are extremely useful professionally. I get perhaps half my sets and characters from dreams. Occasionally I find a book or paper in a dream and read a whole chapter or short story . . . Wake up, make a few notes, sit down at the typewriter the next day, and copy from a dream book.

As soon as we endeavor to describe or define the unconscious we are immediately faced with definitions of conscious which are necessarily misleading, since we have by definition reduced consciousness to a purely verbal and front brain activity. Consciousness is that which defines consciousness. Who is aware of what? Korzybski, who formulated General Semantics, describes consciousness as the reaction of the organism as a whole to its total environment. 'You think as much with your big toe as you do with your brain,' he told his students, 'and a lot more effectively.'

If we postulate that the unconscious is manifested through the non-dominant brain hemisphere we realize that while it may in some cases be a source of pathological and destructive thought and behavior, the non-dominant brain hemisphere is also the source of artistic and creative thought, useful intuitions and ESP faculties, spatial perception, of valuable and essential abilities. It seems evident that consciousness has been so altered since the 19th century partly through therapeutic approaches opened by Freud and his followers, that we now need new terms. Voltaire said of the Holy Roman Empire that it was neither holy, Roman, nor an empire. And the so-called unconscious is no longer unconscious. We are dealing with levels and degrees of awareness. Certain activities require more dominant hemisphere front brain activity than others. In some activities consciousness is a hindrance . . . I quote from a manual on the martial arts . . . 'Once thought no longer becomes necessary, the unified reaction will be attained.'

As regards ESP I think that these abilities and the use of them is very widespread, in fact a part of daily life . . . I recall a former policeman who told me about this telepathic cop. He suddenly for no apparent reason stop and go into a lunch cart and make an arrest. He said he just felt it up through the back of his neck. Others may call it a hunch or a feeling. In face to face it is not possible to separate telepathy from other encounters, other factors, voices, timbre, gestures, facial expression etc. I find that so-called ordinary people are more receptive to ESP experience than intellectuals and scientists, some of whom display an irrational fear and aversion to anything they cannot explain in terms of cause and effect. One scientist said he would never believe in telepathy no matter what evidence was presented.

On Coincidence

From my point of view there is no such thing as a coincidence. But the word is charged with emotional significance. How many times in fiction, when faced by evidence of ESP or any manifestation beyond his rational understanding, the scientist hero cries out.

'*Coincidence*! It has to be! Anything else is unthinkable!'

What is this magic word that exorcises and banishes magic? I turn to Funk and Wagnall's Standard Dictionary. Coincidence: circumstance agreeing with another implying *accident*.

I do not understand exactly why this assertion of randomness produces such a potent sedative effect. It seems to convey a comforting conviction that there is no God in any heaven and what is happening here is no one's plan, intention or responsibility. It *just happened*. Ask why it happened and why just at this particular time and once again the magic word is invoked.

'It was a coincidence.'

The universe is random, Godless and meaningless. Any belief in creators or purpose is wishful thinking. And when you point out that perhaps all thinking is wishful, reactions of intense irritation give evidence that we are dealing not with logic but with faith.

Truth is another highly charged word. However, truth is used to vitalize a statement rather than devitalize it. Truth implies more than a simple statement of fact. 'I don't have any whisky,' may be a fact but it is not a truth.

'What is truth?' said jesting Pilate, and prudently did not stay for an answer. For Christ indeed spoke the truth as enunciated by the Voice of God from the non-dominant brain hemisphere. He spoke with the raw material of which dogmatic truth is made. He spoke with the voice that must be obeyed because it is *there*. Julian Jaynes, in *The Origin of Consciousness in the Breakdown of the Bicameral Brain*, postulates that this voice was once heard by all men and guided human destiny up to about 1000 B.C. The priest-king, he says, was regarded with awe because he had the power to produce his voice in the brains of his loyal subjects. The voice lost power and prestige during a period of chaos, migrations and social upheavals. The voice is still heard by some individuals, but is now regarded as a symptom of mental disorder. To hear that voice is to obey, and so Pilate had as much reason to avoid contact with Christ as he would to avoid a loathsome and highly contagious disease. Many have related the awesome power of the voices, often ordering the subject to commit some violent and dangerous act. We now know that these voices are transmitted from the non-dominant brain hemisphere, and that they can be induced by electric stimulation of the transmitting area in the non-dominant brain hemisphere of normal subjects. Perhaps the voices must be obeyed because they have taken over the motor centers of what is normally voluntary action under control of the dominant brain hemisphere.

As to where the voices came from in the first place and how they gained access to the non-dominant brain hemisphere, that is one of the mysteries. The theory set forth in *2001*, that stranded space travellers took over a tribe of apes, in this way teaching them at the same time to understand and obey the spoken word, seems to me as probable as any other theory I have heard on the origin of language. According to Jaynes's hypothesis, language derived not from practical necessities but from the religious experience. Religious truth is always of a categorical and dogmatic nature. 'I am *the* way and *the* light.' Use of the definite article conveys the concept of one and one only. *The* way. *The* universe. *The* truth. No proof or argument is admissible. Religious truth is *absolute*. Certain individuals seem to have been charged with this truth and able to infect others over thousands of years.

Generations of believers believe because an inner voice tells them that this is the *truth*. And this is a brand of truth as potent as Einstein's great truth: Matter into energy. However, religious truth seems to go in the other direction of grounding energy into matter, that is, into lifeless repetition of dogmatic formulations. Korzybski, who developed the concept of General Semantics, the 'meaning of meaning', points out that Western thought has been crippled by the formulations of Aristotle and Plato. We are still thinking in either/or, absolute terms that don't correspond to what we know about the human nervous system and the physical universe . . . Korzybski would start a lecture by thumping a table . . . 'Whatever this may be it

98

is *not* a table. It is not the verbal label table. We can call it anything so long as we agree that this object is what we are referring to.' Take an abstract word like 'truth'. You can't see it, you can't touch it. Everyone who uses the word has a different definition. Some are referring to religious truth, others to scientific truth, magical truth, pragmatic truth, some to a private lunacy. Everyone is talking at cross purposes. And all this tedium derives from the idea that if you have a label, there must of necessity be something that the label refers to, some absolute essence of truth floating about in a Platonic cave, along with 'good', 'bad', 'justice', and other meaningless abstractions. I am sometimes asked if technology is good; well, for exactly whom, where and when? If you have a clear purpose in mind then you can decide what is good or bad, relative to your purpose. For example you are building a bridge. What leads to getting a workable bridge finished is good. Concepts that result in the bridge falling down are bad. Philosophy, sociology, and psychology tend to founder in verbiage for lack of a clearcut purpose.

Let us consider a variety of truth quite different from the religious variety: the truth of the scientist. At the present time the nearest we can come to an absolute in this area is 186,000 miles per second, the speed of light. Responsible scientists do not hesitate to say that it is 'impossible' to exceed the speed of light, and the word impossible presupposes an absolute standard of possibility. And this absolute in turn presupposes some validity of the measurement tools and the human nervous system that made and recorded the measurements. The so-called scientific method is generally thought to apply to the law of cause and effect. It is however precisely the physical scientists, who have most rigorously examined matter itself, that have punched the first respectable holes in the whole fabric of cause and effect with the inferential discovery of the black hole. The gravity of a black hole traps even light, so that escape is impossible, since escape from the gravity of a black hole would require the impossible, namely, exceeding the speed of light. In a black hole no known natural laws apply. Can we then infer conditions where none of our laws apply including the constant speed of light? Truth in this area seems to end with a question mark.

I will speak now for magical truth to which I myself subscribe. Magic is the assertion of *will*, the assumption that nothing happens in this universe (that is to say the minute

99

fraction of the universe that we are able to contact) unless some entity *wills* it to happen. A magical act is always the triumph or failure of the will.

Among so-called primitive peoples, if a man is killed in a fall from a cliff, the friends and relatives of the victim start looking for a killer.

'This is the work of Izzy the Push,' says the Chief grimly.

Primitive thinking? Perhaps ... In *Psychic Discoveries Behind the Iron Curtain* we meet a Russian psychic who was able, from a distance of a thousand miles, to knock a subject unconscious, by the projected force of his will ... Well, a moment of unconsciousness on a mountain trail ...

It is related that a freelance journalist with papers and pictures in his possession proving CIA involvement in the Bay of Pigs was on his way to keep an appointment with an editor and show him this material. Now it just so happened that the freelance youth was hitchhiking, and it just happened that a CIA man picked him up. The CIA man did everything he could to dissuade the boy from publicizing the material. He failed and called a special number in Washington. On the way to the editor's office the boy was hit and killed by a laundry truck. So that cleaned that up. Murder by car perpetrated during a ten-minute walk through city streets? I recollect the old days in Chicago, when the driver often had to follow the target around for weeks in a souped-up car before he got a clear shot. The Company must have had a way of *pushing* the target in front of the truck ...

The magical push or pull, which potent magic men achieve by a projection of their malignant will, reaches its purest form in defenestration: the subject, standing near a window, is suddenly sucked out, as if a vacuum had opened before him. I suspect that the Company relies on some machine, perhaps a device that projects a hologram. Scientists say that lasers could move satellites in space. Even a little push at just the right moment when the subject is off-guard ... maybe a pretty boy or girl gives him the Company Smile ... just a nudge is all it takes.

Certain pragmatic observations are useful for travellers in the magical universe. One law, or rather expectation, is that lightning usually strikes more than once in the same place.

Here's a big fire in a Kentucky night club, over a hundred dead. Heroic busboy announced the fire and calmed the guests, or the casualties would have been higher. Look through newspaper morgues. Yes, there was a fire in that location before in another night club. No injuries. And here is a night spot on the border between France and Switzerland. Pop group called 'Der Sturm' playing. Two hundred dead in fire. There was a fire there before. Several injured. One incident tends to produce similar incidents. Incident may relate to a place, a set of circumstances, or a person.

You can observe this mechanism operating in your own experience. If you start the day by missing a train, this could be a day of missed trains and missed appointments. You need not just say 'Mektoub, it is written.' The first incident is a warning. Beware of similar incidents. Tighten your schedule. Synchronize your watch. And consider the symbolic meaning of missing a train. Watch particularly for what might be a lost opportunity.

Suppose you encounter a rude clerk, waiter, bartender, elevator man. Shuffle through the morgue of your memory. It's all there. Why he's a dead ringer for a rude clerk in Tangier, London, Hong Kong. Even used the same words. You asked for an item and he said . . .

'I never heard of it.'

Stop. Look. Listen. What were you thinking just before this affront was offered you? What keyed the previous incident in? Empty your mind. Let your legs guide you. You may remember a disinclination to go into that shop in the first place. Stop. Change. Start. You will notice that pleasant encounters with nice friendly helpful people also come in series. And the only valid law of gambling is that winning and losing come in streaks. Plunge when you are winning and stop when you are losing.

'To him that hath shall be given. From him that hath not shall be taken even that which he has.'

Any system in gambling or in life that entails doubling up when you lose is the worst possible system.

Writers operate in the magical universe and you will find the magical law that like attracts like often provides a key note. The sinister clown in *Death in Venice*. The stories of John Cheever abound in such warnings of misfortune and death ignored by his compulsively extroverted and spiritually underprivileged Wasps.

I gave my writing students various exercises designed to show how one incident produces a similar incident or encounter. You can call this process synchronicity and you can observe it in action.

Take a walk around the block. Come back and write down precisely what happened with particular attention to what you were thinking when you noticed a street sign, a passing car or stranger or whatever caught your attention. You will observe that what you were thinking just *before* you saw the sign relates to the sign. The sign may even complete a sentence in your mind. You are getting messages. Everything is talking to you. You start seeing the same person over and over. Are you being followed? At this point some students become paranoid. I tell them that of course they are getting messages. Your surroundings are *your* surroundings. They relate to *you*.

I once read the life story of a leper. Years before he found out that he was going to be a leper he was riding a horse which bolted carrying him straight for a leper colony. Subsequently he turned his leprosy into a profitable part time business raising leprous armadillos for the government research center.

If you can cool it and achieve a detached viewpoint you will see that in many cases incidents are neither good nor bad nor especially potentous, occupying a neutral area. Here I am, up at 72 and Broadway, way out of my neighborhood up there for a doctor appointment. I pass a Deli and decide to go in and get a few items. No stores near where I was then living on Franklin Street below Canal. I notice a young man in the store. Later he is sitting opposite me in the subway going downtown. I see then that we are in the same incident band and I *know* he will get off at Franklin Street. No he wasn't following me. No tail would be that clumsy. We were both out of our neighborhood, both thought of the same thing at the same time . . . Better pick up some . . . and we intersected . . .

There are many variations of the walk exercise all designed to show the student how incidents are created and how he himself can create incidents. Artists and creative thinkers will lead the way into space because they are already writing, painting and filming space. They are providing us with the only maps for space travel. *We are not setting out to explore static pre-existing data*. We are setting out to *create* new worlds, new beings, new modes of consciousness. As Brion Gysin said, when they get there in their trillion dollar aqualungs they may find that artists are already there. The similarity between Brion Gysin's pink picture of a desert landscape and the pictures of Mars sent back by Saturn 11 is immediately apparent to anyone who looks at both pictures. The caption of the Mars picture points out the letter B G on Martian rocks . . . an accident of course carved by wind and sand. In 1963 I wrote '1000 mile per hour wind here, storms . . . crackling sounds . . .

dry and brittle as dead leaves the scouting party climbed a rise and there was our ship half buried in sand.' Years later I heard about the high wind velocities said to exist on the surface of Mars.

What you experience in dreams and out of the body trips, what you glimpse in the work of writers and painters, is the promised land of space. What Christians and Moslems talk about has to be actually *done* by living people if we are going to survive in space or anywhere else.

The shift from time to space may involve mutations as drastic and irreversible as the shift from water to land.

In the beginning was the word and the word *was* God. And what does that make us? Ventriloquist dummies. Time to leave the Word-God behind. 'He atrophied and fell off me like horrible old gills' a survivor reported. 'And I feel ever so much better.'

Paris Please Stay the Same

Maurice Chevalier prances out with his straw hat . . .

> I've seen your mad days
> Some of your sad days
> If I've been happy
> Then you're to blame
> Paris please stay the same

> The last time I saw Paris
> Her heart was young and gay
> No matter how
> They change
> I'll remember her that way

Some time ago a friend conveyed to me the melancholy news that Codethyline Houde would henceforth (owing to the Common Market) be dispensed on prescription only. And I felt the same deep pang of loss as I experienced when they ripped the urinals from the streets, tore down Les Halles, and cut down the trees in the Grand Socco of Tangier and changed the spelling to Tanger. T'is gone, t'is gone . . . another corner of the 19th century . . . brightness falls from the air . . . the urinal, Les Halles, the trees . . .

'Codethyline Houde . . .'

'Oui Monsieur . . . une ou deux?'

'Deux.'

I'll remember her that way.

'The things we have never had remain. It is the things we have that go . . .'

'Maintenant il faut une prescription, Monsieur . . .'

When I think of these passings, they appear to me as if I were looking at something far away and long ago through a telescope. I can see myself propped up in bed, a bottle of little pink pills and science fiction books on the night table, the bones ache and racking cough of Hong Kong flu soothed by this beneficent preparation, squirming with sheer comfort beneath the covers like some 18th-century English gentleman who has taken to his bed for the winter. And I remember when I still had the habit after a day in jail . . .

Pharmacie . . . green neon letters in electric blue twilight . . . washed down twenty-four pinkies with a café crême, then it hit the back of my neck and crept down the backs of my thighs and there was this Edith Piaf number on the jukebox . . .

You can hear my goodbye
In the whistle of the train . . .

And I remember Les Halles, not as I saw it in the Fifties and Sixties, but as I saw it on my first solo trip to Europe at age eighteen after a night of drinking . . . onion soup, smell of sawdust, red wine, urine and bread . . . The cab driver who parked his cab and asked me into a bar for a drink. He was talking about the Stavinsky riots: 'Et tout d'un coup . . . Bthruuuuuuuup' (a sound like ripping cloth) When you hear machine guns you know its serious . . . (knowing laugh of the dead)

On n'est pas sérieux
Quand on a dix-sept ans

It is fall and there are dead leaves in the street . . . somewhere around Auteuil . . . a long wall . . .

'Simon, aimes-tu le bruit des pas sur les feuilles mortes?' Simon, do you like the sound of footsteps on dead leaves? Dead leaves drifting into the pissoir, sharp ammonia reek of urine . . . there on the galvanized iron, words that could have been written by Rimbaud: 'J'aime ces type vicieux, q'ici montre la bite' — I like the vicious types who show their cocks here . . . Un soldat jeune, tres jeune, glances sideways . . . Oh la la . . . Well t'is gone t'is gone . . .

I can see the old opium peddler there under a tree in the Grand Socco, his gold teeth glinting in the sun. Jane Bowles got up a petition to save the trees and that old bitch Madame Porte, who ran the Porte Tea Room, refused to sign, saying: 'Je n'ai pas une opinion.' I do not have an opinion.

It is the things we have that go . . . the urinals . . . Les Halles . . . the trees . . . Tangier . . . Codethyline Houde . . .

You can hear good bye
In the whistle of the train
N'existe plus
Il pleut dans la ville
Finnies nous attendons bonne chance
'It is raining Miss Charrington.'

Codethyline Houde . . . A preparation of dehydrated codeine sold across the counter in France until the recent ruling —

> T'is gone, t'is gone . . . *Romeo and Juliet*
> Brightness falls from the air . . . poem by Thomas Nash
> 'For I have lived enough to know/ The things we never had remain/ It is the things we have that go . . . Sara Teasdale, St. Louis poetess, who drowned herself many years ago, circa 1933
> Knowing laugh of the dead . . . rire savant des mortes . . . *Anabase* by Saint-John Perse
> 'On n'est pas serieux/ Quand on a dix-sept ans.' One is not serious when one is seventeen . . . Rimbaud
> 'Il pleut dans mon coeur
> Comme il pleut dans la ville'
> It rains in my heart
> as it rains in the city . . . Verlaine

Finnies nous attendons bonne chance . . . Quite a story connected with this. In 1960 four young men got together in Paris and bought a Land Rover to cross the Libyan desert. Their names were Armstrong, Shannon, Pelieu and Yves Martin. The first two were American, the other two French. They picked up a guide in Aswan near the Sudan border. Months later an Egyptian patrol found the stalled Land Rover. Four corpses were in or near the car, but advanced decomposition made identification difficult. Who was missing? Was it the guide? The Egyptians said it was Shannon. A diary was found in the car and this is the last entry . . .

> Finnies nous attendons la chance . . .
> Finished we await good luck

Ungrammatical French would suggest that one of the Americans made the entry. A chapter in *The Soft Machine* entitled 'Back Seat of Dreaming' was based on this incident.

'It is raining Miss Charrington . . .' Last words of Ulysses S. Grant spoken to his nurse.

God's Own Medicine

Poppy field on screen... the petals fall like snow in the wind...

Commentator voice: 'The opium poppy has been cultivated for thousands of years and opium extracted from the ripening seed pods.' As he says this we see workers emptying little scoops of opium into a cauldron of water.

'The juice drained from the pods is boiled and filtered to remove impurities, then processed into raw opium.' — Blocks of opium on screen — 'And for thousands of years opium has brought relief to suffering humanity — suffering from the pains of sickness . . .' — persons in various costumes from togas to suits take opium in one form or another for coughs, colds, lumbago, toothache, leprosy, etc. — 'The pain of old age . . .' — Old Chinese smoking opium — 'The pain of grinding poverty . . .' — Indian farmers in a hovel wash down opium at dawn — 'Or the pain of simple boredom.'

Eighteenth-century gentleman in chemist's shop; Chemist: 'Shocking night out sir.'

Gentleman: 'Yes indeed. Need a spot of laudanum.'

Chemist: 'Certainly sir. How much?'

Gentleman: 'A litre. Taking to my bed for the winter you know.'

Chemist: 'Of course sir. Very sensible of you sir.'

(Commentator continues:) 'Armies have marched on opium from Vietnam to Asia Minor a thousand years ago.' A soldier in Vietnam leans his M-16 against a tree and takes a shot . . . same soldier in Turkish dress washes down his ration of opium, dates, and brown sugar.

'But long before the poppy was brought under cultivation and man learned to extract the opium, some intrepid experimenter must have eaten an opium pod, discovered its medicinal properties, and passed this knowledge along to apprentices. Here are the Unglings, a Cro-Magnon tribe 30,000 years ago. Homo sapiens like you and me — or the folks next door.'

The prehistoric Unglings are in animal skins, carrying stone

107

axes; one is old, suffering from rheumatism, hobbling along with the aid of a staff. They come to a field of opium poppies. The petals have fallen and the pods are ripe and yellow. The old man can go no further. He sinks down among the pods. One hands rolls a pod in his fingers; there is a speculative look on his face. He bites into the pod, sucking the juice. He gets up and throws away his staff. Vigorously he directs the others as they gather pods.

'Throughout the long cold winter the Unglings take refuge in a cave, cooking the pods into thick black brew. It is a bitter potion, but somehow it makes it easier to endure the cold, the hunger, the endless search for food.'

The Unglings pass around the gourd of opium solution. They shudder at the bitterness but then smile as the potion takes effect, and go vigorously about their tasks.'

'But unexpected things were happening . . .' A female Ungling, hands on hips, stands over a young male. She breaks into vituperative words. 'What is she saying? Well I think we can all guess . . . and now something else: as spring comes on and the last of the pods have been used, the Unglings are suddenly very sick. What is this mysterious illness that afflicts not only the old but also the young? Can nothing be done? The wise old Ungling has an inspiration. There must, he thinks, be some connection between the lack of pods and the illness. Young Unglings are dispatched. They return with pods. And soon the old man's wisdom is manifest.'

Over the years countless millions were to confirm the findings of the wise old Ungling, and to learn that opium affords relief from pain, discomfort, illness and fatigue, but exacts over a period of time the price of dependence. Four to six months' daily use establishes addiction, and the sudden withdrawal of opium then brings on a spectrum of incapacitating symptoms: stomach cramps and diarrhea, watering of the eyes and nose, sneezing fits, restlessness and insomnia, weakness and prostration, hypersensitivity, spontaneous orgasms, and nightmares.

Cocteau likened withdrawal symptoms to the spurting flow of sap into the trees. Yet at the same time there is a feeling of renewal and increased health; Thomas De Quincey wrote: 'Jeremy Taylor conjectures that it may be as painful to be born as to die, and during the whole period of diminishing opium I had the torments of a man passing from one mode of existence to another. The issue was not death but a sort of physical regeneration, and a restoration of more than youthful spirits.' (The experience of withdrawal has never been more precisely or succinctly stated.)

De Quincey has written a detailed and accurate account of the opium experience in his *Confessions of an English Opium Eater*; and I invite all those who have shared the whole or any part of this experience, if only a pre- or post-operative injection of morphine or a percodan for a toothache, to enter into the mind and body of a 19-year-old English youth on a rainy Sunday in London.

The date is September 17, 1804. De Quincey has wandered forth from his digs, in great pain from facial neuralgia brought on by an infected tooth. Walking seemingly at random, he finds himself in front of a modest tea house, which he enters. He recognizes an acquaintance from Oxford, Audrey Lawson, and sits down with him. When his tea arrives he cannot control a spasm of pain from the hot liquid on his tooth. His friend inquires as to his difficulty, and listens sympathetically.

'I would recommend a tincture of opium. My great-aunt was in great pain from shingles, and obtained complete relief from the use of this remedy.'

Walking home along Oxford Street, De Quincey sees a light in a chemist's shop. The rain has abated, to be followed by a heavy fog, and fog drifts into the chemist's shop as he opens the door. A ghostly druggist looks at him absently.

'Do you have a tincture of opium?'

'Laudanum? Certainly sir.' His movements are unhurried and old as he fills a small bottle. He gives change for a shilling. 'Twenty-five drops every four to six hours sir.'

Back in his lodgings, young De Quincey measures out 35 drops. He drinks the draught, lights a fire in the grate, and sits down. He will later write that the dreams and visions of opium are like to those of a drowning man when his entire life passes before his eyes . . .

'Let there be a cottage in a valley, a white cottage embowered with flowering shrubs. Let it however not be spring, summer, or autumn but winter. Paint me then a room seventeen feet by twelve . . .' De Quincey sits by the fire drinking tea, with which he washes down a carefully measured dose of laudanum from a decanter.

De Quincey has catalogued the opium experience with an accuracy and a candor that has never been surpassed; even noting the metabolic predisposition to addiction recently confirmed by research into endorphin, a natural pain-killer produced by the brain. He has described, under the section entitled 'The Pains of Opium', the extreme melancholy and continual nightmares that can accompany heavy over-dosage. His nightmares involved evil Oriental faces and scenes. He describes withdrawal symptoms and how opium can be gradually withdrawn, a system that is used to this day. He remarks the extreme difficulty of withdrawal carried out by the addict himself, who will always find some excuse for an exception. During fifty years he was only free of opium use for one period of six months and one period of four months.

On the whole, one cannot but feel that he was better off for using opium than he would have been without it, and he says that without opium he would have died from consumption at an early age. At that time the use and purchase of opium were quite legal, and even though he was criticized on moral grounds, no one questioned his right to buy and use opium. Some of this criticism came from Coleridge, and after Coleridge died in 1834, De Quincey, in the revised *Opium Eater* written when he was 70 years old, provides this amusing account of Coleridge's unsuccessful attempts to overcome the opium habit:

'It is notorious that in Bristol he went so far as to hire men — porters, hackney-coachmen, and others — to oppose by force his entrance into any druggist's shop. But, as the authority for stopping him was derived simply from himself, these poor men found themselves in a metaphysical fix, not provided for even by the prince of Jesuitical casuists.

'*Porter*: "Oh sir, really you must not; consider, sir, your wife and —"

'*Coleridge*: "Wife! What wife? I have no wife!"

'*Porter*: "But, really now, you must not, sir. Didn't you say no longer ago than yesterday —"

'*Coleridge*: "Pooh, pooh. Yesterday is a long time ago. Are you aware, my man, that people are known to have dropped down *dead* for timely want of opium?"

'*Porter*: "Ay, but you tell't me not to hearken —"

'*Coleridge*: "No matter what I told you in times long passed. An emergency, a shocking emergency, has arisen — quite unlooked for."'

And so we take leave of Thomas De Quincey, Esquire, with his laudanum, his tea, his books and papers. In his *Confessions* he describes a dream from which he awoke with the phrase 'everlasting farewells' echoing in his mind. And such farewells are never taken without a deep feeling of nostalgia. Winter evenings, a cheery fire, candlelight on the ruby red decanter of laudanum.

The Last Junky

A.J. closes the folder and puts his elbow on it, leaning forward. He looks at B.J. with cold disfavor.

A.J.: 'Frankly we don't like to hear the word '*last*' around the Studio — 'last' *anything* . . . What's the Weenie, B.J.?' (Note: The 'Weenie,' the 'Macguff,' the 'gimmick,' the 'routine,' are all Hollywood lingo for the formula, the map, the deed, or whatever it is that motivates the action of a film: what everybody is trying to get or hang onto.)

B.J.: 'What if a sure one-shot cure for drug addiction is discovered? And what if not only the Mafia and other organized dope dealers, but also the American Narcotics Department and the CIA attempt to block this discovery by any means, however execrable? You got a neat switcheroo on the clean-cut agents chasing slimy traffickers. Here the agents *and* the slimy traffickers are united against this threat to their common livelihood.'

A.J.: 'All right so far . . . the ground is already broken by Watergate and *The Marathon Man* . . .'

B.J.: 'It must be made clear at the outset that the possibility of an effective cure has actually existed for some time, and has so far been successfully blocked by the above-named interested parties. A brief account of the apomorphine cure as introduced by Doctor Dent of London, the combination of apomorphine and L-dopa now successfully used in Denmark, and acupuncture . . . a certain amount of technical information which must be conveyed to the audience in a simple, interesting, and novel form. The recent discovery that all vertebrates, even the most primitive fish and reptiles, have opiate receptors in their brains and are in consequence susceptible to addiction — (I got a great running gag here A.J. about addicted dinosaurs) — well this discovery of opiate receptors led scientists to the supposition that the body manufactures a substance similar to morphine, which is released in the body in response to pain, tension and anxiety. In the event of massive injury and acute pain, this substance is not produced rapidly enough or in sufficient quantity to counteract bodily defense reactions, leading in many cases to circulatory collapse, shock, and death.

'As soon as scientists inferred the presence of a morphine-like substance produced by the body itself, they set out to isolate this substance. A Doctor Goldstein has isolated a substance he calls Pituitary Opioid Peptide — P.O.P. We now have a more precise formulation of the mechanism of withdrawal. When morphine or heroin is taken over a period of time, the body ceases to produce P.O.P., which is no longer needed. And when the morphine or heroin is then cut off, the body is without its natural painkiller — so that what would ordinarily be scarcely noticeable discomfort, owing to the action of this natural painkiller and regulator, now becomes intolerable until the body again produces the P.O.P. Scientists have suggested that acupuncture may work on addicts by stimulating the production of P.O.P.

'We can further surmise that apomorphine, which is made by boiling morphine with hydrochloric acid but has no painkilling but addicting properties, acts directly on the opiate receptors to stimulate the renewed production of P.O.P., which therefore leads to quicker recovery, although the recovery is by no means immediate or devoid of discomfort. Now suppose we treat P.O.P. with hydrochloric acid to obtain a *super-regulator*, which restores the production of natural P.O.P. and normal metabolism with a single injection? *And suppose this cure is actually announced as the film is released?* How about *that* for P.R.?'

A.J.: 'Yeah, how about it? Next thing the Industry gets blamed for fires and monsters and epidemics and earthquakes . . . We can do without P.R. like that.'

B.J.: 'A number of questions must be answered before our film —'

A.J.: '*Your* film, B.J.'

B.J.: 'Well, the film has to be logical and believable. Research on the isolation of the P.O.P. is underway, and has been reported in scientific journals and the public media. No doubt some of this research is in fact government-sponsored. How then can such research be stopped, without creating a monster scandal which would be picked up by the media? Well, we postulate a super international commando team of narcs, CIA, Mafia, Chinese, Blacks and Mexicans: ruthless, well-financed, prepared to stop at nothing. We outline methods of attack: actual sabotage of laboratories while spreading the story that the Chinese Communists are the perpetrators and their motive to protect their worldwide drug-smuggling operations; setting up dummy laboratories to deliberately produce negative results; blocking the drug from release by 'demonstrating' falsified dangers; in some cases murdering key scientists by poisons that cannot be detected. These measures our commandos consider adequate in the absence of organized opposition.

'However, organized opposition is on the way. This consists of the English doctor who developed the apomorphine treatment and has striven for many years to obtain acceptance for this treatment, which could lead to synthesis and potentiation of the apomorphine formula. He has cured two addicts who are former double secret agents and knows the ins and outs of cloak-and-dagger operations, and who have seen the American Narcotics Department in operation. These two start to line up the opposing team: an idealistic ex-doctor from Lexington, ex-narcs, and pushers. The opposing team will contain representatives of all ethnic groups.

'The operation is financed by an eccentric billionaire who intends to make money on the cure drug. The research of course will have to be conducted underground. So instead of a West Indian island or a remote mountain hideaway, they set up the lab in a New York SoHo loft. The cover is modern art and underground films. We can pass off our apparatus as art objects. This is a running gag and spoof on modern art, and gives us a cheap location in which a number of scenes can be shot.

'Soon, of course, the commando team realizes that they have opposition. The actual drug turns out to be more complicated than just treating P.O.P. with hydrochloric acid, but they are getting closer and closer — and as the film reaches its climax, we find out just how far the commando team is prepared to go: they will start a World War by dropping an atom bomb on New York.

"Gentlemen, the entire future of behavior modification is at stake. If this devilish drug ever hits the open market, everything we have striven for will be lost. *Irretrievably* lost . . ." And then your count-down climax.'

A.J.: 'Not too bad . . . you spoke of presenting technical data to the audience in an acceptable form. Just how do you propose to do this?'

B.J.: 'I'm glad you asked me that question, A.J. The back-up

114

on this film is a 15- or 20-minute documentary on the history of opium, opium use, anti-opium legislation, with an exposé of the American Narcotics Department and the so-called Hospital at Lexington, Kentucky. You see it's a *package*: a film *and* a documentary giving a run-down on the material in the film.'

A.J.: 'You got any more ideas like that, B.J.?'

B.J.: 'Sure, lots of them.'

A.J.: 'You remember the Humphrey Bogart movie, *High Sierra*? Bogart plays the last of the big-time heist men, just out of prison and planning a big caper with two small-time punks. One of the punks is telling the story about a liquor store holdup: "So we lam out the back way and the cops have the alley blocked at both ends." Bogart just looks at him and says: "You know any more stories like that?"

'So you got a documentary on the American Narcotics Department, right? And that goes with the film. So everyone in the film can be clearly identified and we get hit with a billion-dollar libel suit . . . Not that the idea is totally impractical . . . Hmmm, yes, a documentary that goes with the film . . . that way a lot of information that has to be awkwardly introduced, clogging the action and boring the audience, can be conveyed in the documentary. Suppose we want to do a film on *The Anthrax Mutation* by Alan Scott; we start with a documentary called *"Anthrax and You"*.'

B.J.: '"*Moooooooo . . .*" I get it . . . a chorus of bellowing cows; a folksy down-to-earth explanation by a wise old veterinarian; an animation sequence on Mr Anthrax, and how he gets drafted by the Army into a top-secret laboratory, and how he goes AWOL . . . That way we don't have the scene where two doctors working on the same project have to tell each other in simple non-technical language what the project is all about.'

A.J.: 'The whole concept has to be kept under control and used in non-controversial areas . . .'

B.J.: 'Well, it's all a matter of how you slant it. On this narco-doc film we simply explain to the audience in simple terms about junk and addiction, and we *show* the audience what the Department is doing with the taxpayers' money . . . "By their fruits ye shall know them"'

A.J.: '"If the condom fits . . ."'

The Limits of Control

There is a growing interest in new techniques of mind-control. It has been suggested that Sirhan Sirhan was the subject of post-hypnotic suggestion [as he sat shaking violently on the steam table in the kitch of the Ambassador Hotel in Los Angeles while an as-yet unidentified woman held him and whispered in his ear]. It has been alleged that behavior-modification techniques are used on troublesome prisoners and inmates, often without their consent. Dr Delgado, who once stopped a charging bull by remote control of electrodes in the bull's brain, left the U.S. to pursue his studies on human subjects in Spain. Brainwashing, psychotropic drugs, lobotomy and other more subtle forms of psychosurgery; the technocratic control apparatus of the United States has at its fingertips new techniques which if fully exploited could make Orwell's 1984 seem like a benevolent utopia. But words are still the principal instruments of control. Suggestions are words. Persuasions are words. Orders are words. No control machine so far devised can operate without words, and any control machine which attempts to do so relying entirely on external force or entirely on physical control of the mind will soon encounter the limits of control.

A basic impasse of all control machines is this: Control needs time in which to exercise control. Because control also needs opposition or acquiescence; otherwise it ceases to be control. I *control* a hypnotized subject (at least partially); I *control* a slave, a dog, a worker; but if I establish *complete* control somehow, as by implanting electrodes in the brain, then my subject is little more than a tape recorder, a camera, a robot. You don't *control* a tape recorder — you *use* it. Consider the distinction, and the impasse implicit here. All control systems try to make control as tight as possible, but at the same time, if they succeeded completely, there would be nothing left to control. Suppose for example a control system installed electrodes in the brains of all prospective workers at birth. Control is now complete. Even the thought of rebellion is neurologically impossible. No police force is necessary. No psychological control is necessary, other than pressing buttons to achieve certain activations and operations.

When there is no more opposition, control becomes a meaningless proposition. It is highly questionable whether a human organism could survive complete control. There would be nothing there. No persons there. *Life is will* (motivation) and the workers would no longer be alive, perhaps literally. The concept of suggestion as a control technique presupposes that control is partial and not complete. You do not have to give suggestions to your tape-recorder, nor subject it to pain and coercion or persuasion.

In the Mayan control system, where the priests kept the all-important Books of seasons and gods, the Calendar was predicated on the illiteracy of the workers. Modern control systems are predicated on universal literacy since they operate through the mass media — a very two-edged control instrument, as Watergate has shown. Control systems are vulnerable, and the news media are by their nature uncontrollable, at least in western society. The alternative press is news, and alternative society is news, and as such both are taken up by the mass media. The monopoly that Hearst and Luce once exercised is breaking down. In fact, the more completely hermetic and seemingly successful a control system is, the more vulnerable it becomes. A weakness inherent in the Mayan system is that they didn't need an army to control their workers, and therefore did not have an army when they needed one to repel invaders. It is a rule of social structures that anything that is not needed will atrophy and become inoperative over a period of time. Cut off from the war game — and remember, the Mayans had no neighbors to quarrel with — they lose the ability to fight. In The Mayan Caper I suggested that such a hermetic control system could be completely disoriented and shattered by even one person who tampered with the control calendar on which the control system depended more and more heavily as the actual means of force withered away.

Consider a control situation: ten people in a lifeboat. Two armed self-appointed leaders force the other eight to do the rowing while they dispose of the food and water, keeping most of it for themselves and doling out only enough to keep the other eight rolling. The two leaders now *need* to exercise control to maintain an advantageous position which they could not hold without it. Here the method of control is force — the possession

117

of guns. Decontrol would be accomplished by overpowering the leaders and taking their guns. This effected, it would be advantageous to kill them at once. So once embarked on a policy of control, the leaders must continue the policy as a matter of self-preservation. Who, then, needs to control others but those who protect by such control a position of relative advantage? Why do they need to exercise control? Because they would soon lose this position and advantage and in many cases their lives as well, if they relinquished control.

Now examine the reasons by which control is exercised in the lifeboat scenario: The two leaders are armed, let's say, with .38 revolvers — twelve shots and eight potential opponents. They can take turns sleeping. However, they must still exercise care not to let the eight rowers know that they intend to kill them when land is sighted. Even in this primitive situation force is supplemented with deception and persuasion. The leaders will disembark at point A, leaving the others sufficient food to reach point B, they explain. They have the compass and they are contributing their navigational skills. In short they will endeavour to convince the others that this is a cooperative enterprise in which they are all working for the same goal. They may also make concessions: increase food and water rations. A concession of course means the retention of control — that is, the disposition of the food and water supplies. By persuasions and by concessions they hope to prevent a concerted attack by the eight rowers.

Actually they intend to poison the drinking water as soon as they leave the boat. If all the rowers knew this they would attack, no matter what the odds. We now see that another essential factor in control is to conceal from the controlled the actual intentions of the controllers. Extending the lifeboat analogy to the Ship of State, few existing governments could withstand a sudden, all-out attack by all their underprivileged citizens, and such an attack might well occur if the intentions of certain existing governments were unequivocally apparent. Suppose the lifeboat leaders had built a barricade and could withstand a concerted attack and kill all eight of the rowers if necessary. They would then have to do the rowing themselves and neither would be safe from the other. Similarly, a modern government armed with heavy weapons and prepared for attack could wipe out ninety-five percent of its citizens. But who would do the work, and who would protect them from the soldiers and technicians needed to make and man the weapons? Successful

118

control means achieving a balance and avoiding a showdown where all-out force would be necessary. This is achieved through various techniques of psychological control, also balanced. The techniques of both force and psychological control are constantly improved and refined, and yet worldwide dissent has never been so widespread or so dangerous to the present controllers.

All modern control systems are riddled with contradictions. Look at England. 'Never go too far in any direction,' is the basic rule on which England is built, and there is some wisdom in that. However, avoiding one impasse they step into another. Anything that is not going forward is on the way out. Well, nothing lasts forever. Time is that which ends, and control needs time. England is simply stalling for time as it slowly founders. Look at America. Who actually controls this country? It is very difficult to say. Certainly the very wealthy are one of the most powerful control groups, since they are in a position to control and manipulate the entire economy. However, it would not be to their advantage to set up or attempt to set up an overly fascist government. Force, once brought in, subverts the power of money. This is another impasse of control: protection from the protectors. Hitler formed the S.S. to protect him from the S.A. If he had lived long enough the question of protection from the S.S. would have posed itself. The Roman Emperors were at the mercy of the Pretorian Guard, who in one year killed many Emperors. And besides, no modern industrial country has ever gone fascist without a program of military expansion. There is no longer anyplace to expand to — after hundreds of years, colonialism is a thing of the past.

There can be no doubt that a cultural revolution of unprecedented dimensions has taken place in America during the last thirty years, and since America is now the model for the rest of the Western world, this revolution is worldwide. Another factor is the mass media, which spreads all cultural movements in all directions. The fact that this worldwide revolution has taken place indicates that the controllers have been forced to make concessions. Of course, a concession is still the retention of control. Here's a dime, I keep a dollar. Ease up on censorship, but remember we could take it all back. Well, at this point, that is questionable.

Concession is another control bind. History shows that once a government starts to make concessions it is on a one-way street. They could of course take all the concessions back, but that would expose them to the double jeopardy of revolution and the much greater danger of overt fascism, both highly dangerous to the present controllers. Does any clear policy arise from this welter of confusion? The answer is probably no. The mass media has proven a very unreliable and even treacherous instrument of control. It is uncontrollable owing to its need for NEWS. If one paper or even a string of papers owned by the same person, makes that story hotter as NEWS, some paper will pick it up. Any imposition of government censorship on the media is a step in the direction of State control, a step which big money is most reluctant to take.

I don't mean to suggest that control automatically defeats itself, nor that protest is therefore unnecessary. A government is never more dangerous than when embarking on a self-defeating or downright suicidal course. It is encouraging that some behavior modification projects have been exposed and halted, and certainly such exposure and publicity could continue. In fact, I submit that we have a *right* to insist that all scientific research be subject to public scrutiny, and that there should be no such thing as 'top-secret' research.

The Hundred Year Plan

Communism was conceived as a reaction against 19th century *laissez faire* capitalism, to oppose an economic and political system that no longer exists today.

Dialectical materialism is an ideological formulation and precisely because of its materialistic pretentions it cannot adjust to change. The West has come a long way from Daddy Warbucks and the better mouse trap. It has come a long way from sweat shops, child labor and starvation wages. The corporate structure of Western Capitalism has no more use for the small operator with a better car, house, gun, fabric or contraceptive pill. Nor can it afford to tolerate such abuses as accompanied old style capitalism. Since it has no ideology it can adjust to altered conditions. But it lacks a long range plan. All such plans require an ideology, and it does not matter if the ideology is faulty, illogical, outmoded or proven wrong again and again. What matters is that a substantial body of Soviet citizens believe it and put the state above the individual. And what does the Soviet State intend? Exactly what they say they intend: world conquest. We will bury you and turn your graves into fertile asparagus beds to feed our workers. We need only one million brown nosed Afghans to found the socialist state. The other eleven million must be dealt with as enemies of the people, cod-eyed buffoons dedicated to counter-revolutionary obstructionist hooliganism.

The words don't matter. What matters is Russian planes and tanks and guns and Russian soldiers ready to deal with cod-eyed buffoons on an assembly line basis and plough them under for the collective farms that will feed our workers.

Is it reactionary to repeat what they themselves have said? Of course they intend world conquest. What else? It's all there in Marx. Next move Mid-East oil. Check. Anybody going to get tactical? *Qui vivra verra.*

I'm an elitist. I believe in government by those able to govern. There are very few people who are good at anything, very few good lawyers, doctors, carpenters, writers, painters.

Politics is the only area where stupidity and ignorance are brazenly proffered as qualification for office . . . I stand here a plain blunt man talking with no Groton accents.

Limit the right to vote . . . those who obtain power are the least competent to use it. This is a *wanting* universe. They get it because they want it, whatever it is, shoving aside the worthy bidden guest. The whole majority-rule farce is a door through which the unworthy enter, knowing that a select and discriminating instance would relegate them to the menial and clerical jobs they might be able to perform . . . You do not enhance the survival potential of a species by handing all basic decisions over to the unfit, those who are least competent to represent that species.

Politics is the only area where stupidity and ignorance are brazenly proffered as qualifications for office . . . Foote said he didn't want to hear the facts about marijuana use, having already made up his mind . . . Or Wendell Willkie: 'I stand here a plain blunt man with no Groton accent . . .' Intelligence, learning are words of reproach . . . 'egg heads'!

And so, guided by the least intelligent, the least competent, the least farsighted and most ill-informed, the species invites biologic disaster . . . Other species have come and gone . . .

Consider the dinosaurs . . . A beast fifty feet in length and weighing thousands of tons, with a brain the size of a walnut . . . He had grave problems, but he could not worry . . . Many theories have been advanced as to why these magnificent creatures disappeared . . . Certainly one factor was size . . . The carnivorous models were so large that the problem of obtaining adequate nourishment posed a chronic problem which over the centuries and the millennia must have become acute.

One herbivorous species was equipped with thin long necks that become longer and longer to reach more and more fodder, they may have reached an impasse where even if they ate day and night they could not sustain their way of life . . . There was also the problem posed by emergent mammalian creatures eating their eggs, thus striking at the very roots of their survival . . . Let us imagine a congress and emergency meeting of the dinosaur leaders. The brightest and the best . . . or so they see themselves . . .

'Fellow reptiles, at this dark hour, I do not hesitate to tell you that we face grave problems . . . And I do not hesitate to tell you that we have the answer . . . Size is the answer . . . increased size . . . It was good enough for me . . . (Applause) Size that will enable us to crush all opposition (Applause) . . . There are those who say size is not the answer. There are those who even propose that we pollute our pure reptilian strain with mammalian amalgamations and cross breeding . . . And I say to you that if the only way I could survive was by mating with egg-eating rats, then I would choose not to survive . . . (Applause). But we *will* survive . . . We *will* increase both in size and in numbers and we will continue to dominate this planet as we have done for three hundred million years . . . (Wild applause).

And this is what we are seeing and hearing at the present time . . . At the time when the greatest diversity, and biologic flexibility moving towards mutation is needed for survival, we see a demand for increased conformity and standardization both in the West and in the Communist countries.

Intelligence and war are games, perhaps the only meaningful games left. If any player becomes too proficient, the game is threatened with termination. Like the karate man who could slice the top off a beer bottle leaving the bottle standing. He was never in an actual fight — who would fight him? And the phenomenal gun artists like Joe MacGivern were never in a gun fight . . . They were too good . . .

If intelligence is one of the last games, then proficiency must be carefully, uh, rationed . . . That is why intelligence agencies are reluctant to use polygraphs, except to weed out queers and drug addicts in their own ranks . . . Here is a spy novel by Le Carré called *The Spy Who Came in from the Cold* . . . Leamas is a false defector to the Communists, pretending to be disgruntled by the treatment meted out to him by British intelligence . . . Incidentally one of the oldest ploys in the intelligence game, the apparent defector . . . How long would he last on a polygraph?

So the Johnsons have an incalculable advantage. They aren't playing. They want to end the whole stupid game. To us, intelligence and war are only means to an end: SPACE EXPLORATION.

Women: A Biological Mistake?

I realize I am widely perceived as a misogynist. But quoting from the Oxford dictionary: 'Misogynist — a woman hater.' Presumably this is his full-time occupation? Korzybski, the founder of General Semantics, always said to pin a generality down; so *what* women? Where and when? My English nanny from the pages of 'The Turn of the Screw?' She did teach me some useful jingles — 'Trip and stumble, slip and fall . . .' Or the old Irish crone who taught me how to call the toads and bring the blinding worm from rotten bread? How remote and nostalgic with a whiff of peat and pigsties. Or the Saint Louis matron who said I was a walking corpse? Well, it isn't every corpse that can walk; hers can't.

Bring on the heavies. The *femme fatale*, in all her guises . . . Kali does her sideshow coochy dance . . . the White Goddess eats her consort . . . the Terrible Mother goes into her act . . . the whore of Babylon rides in on her black panther screaming, 'You fools! I will drain you dry.' Enough to turn a man to stone. But these are only surface manifestations, B-girls in fact: servants. After one look at this planet any visitor from outer space would say 'I WANT TO SEE THE *MANAGER*.'

Women may well be a biological mistake; I said so in *The Job*. But so is almost everything else I see around here. The dinosaurs turned out to be a mistake too, but what are a few hundred million years, more or less, for such a noble experiment? And now — as the deadly cycles of overpopulation, pollution, depletion of resources, radio-activity and conflict escalate towards a cataclysmic *sauve-qui-peut* — thoughtful citizens are asking themselves if the whole human race wasn't a mistake from the starting gate. The question then arises as to *whose* mistake, since mistakes imply intention — and I am convinced that nothing happens in this universe without will or intention.

Now it would be presumptuous, not to say impious, to say the Creator has done a bad job; since a bad job from *our* point of view may be a good job from his or her or its point of view. The history of the planet is a history of idiocy highlighted by a few morons who stand out as comparative geniuses. Considering the human organism as the *artifact* of an intentional Creator, we can then see more or less where we are. To date, no super-genius has managed to achieve what might be called normal intelligence in terms of the potential functioning of the human artifact.

'Look at this artifact.' The instructor holds up a flintlock rifle. 'What's wrong with it? Quite a bit. It still has a long way to go.'

He holds up a modern automatic rifle. 'Now we are getting close to the limit of efficiency for small arms on the principle of a projectile propelled by an exploding charge. Now look at *this* artifact.' He holds up a cage in which a weasel snarls. 'What's wrong with this artifact? Nothing. It's limited, but in terms of its structure and goals it functions well enough . . .'

Take a look at the human artifact. What is wrong with it? Just about everything. Consider a species that can live on the seacoast, watching ships come in day after day, year after year, and still believe that the Earth is flat because the Church says so; a species that can use cannonballs for five hundred years before the idea of a cannonball that explodes on contact blossoms in this barren soil . . . I could go on and on. So why has the human artifact stayed back there with the flintlock? I am advancing a theory that we were not designed to remain in our present state, any more than a tadpole is designed to remain a tadpole forever.

The human organism is in a state of neoteny. This is a biological term used to describe an organism fixated at what would normally be a larval or transitional phase. Ordinarily a salamander starts its life cycle in the water with gills; later the gills atrophy, and the animal develops lungs. However, certain salamanders never lose their gills or leave the water. They are in a state of neoteny. The Xolotl salamander found in Mexico is an example. Scientists, moved by the plight of this beautiful creature, gave him an injection of hormones, whereupon he shed his gills and left the water after ages of neoteny. It is perhaps too much to hope that one simple injection could jar the human species out of its neoteny. But by whatever means the change takes place, it will be irreversible. The Xolotl, once he sheds his gills, can never reclaim them. Evolution would seem to be a one way street.

Considering evolutionary steps, one has the feeling that the creature is tricked into making them. Here is a fish that survives drought because it has developed feet or rudimentary lungs. So far as the fish is concerned, these are simply a means of getting from one water source to another. But once he leaves his gills behind, he is stuck with lungs from there on out. So the fish has made an evolutionary step forward. Looking for water, he has found air.

Perhaps a forward step for the human race will be made in the same way. The astronaut is not looking for space; he is looking for more *time* — that is, equating space with time. The space program is simply an attempt to transport our insoluble temporal impasses somewhere else. However, like the walking fish, looking for more time we may find space instead, and then find that there is no way back.

Such an evolutionary step would involve changes that are literally inconceivable from our present point of view. Is the separation of the sexes an arbitrary device to perpetuate an unworkable arrangement? Would the next step involve the sexes fusing into an organism? And what would be the nature of this organism? As Korzybski always said, 'I don't know. Let's see.' Is it too much to ask that this beached fish of a species — the human race — should consider the unthinkable, for evolution's sake?

Immortality

'To me the only success the only greatness is immortality.' James Dean
Quote from *James Dean the Mutant King* by David Dalton

The colonel beams at the crowd . . . pomaded, manicured, he wears the satisfied expression of one who has just sold the widow a fraudulent peach orchard. 'Folks we're here to sell the only thing worth selling or buying and that's immortality. Now here is the simplest solution and well on the way. Just replace the worn parts and keep the old heap on the road indefinitely.'

As transplant techniques are perfected and refined the age-old dream of immortality is now within the grasp of mankind. But who is to decide out of a million applicants for the same heart? There simply aren't enough parts to go around. You need the job-lot once a year save twenty percent of people applying. Big executives use a heart a month just as regular as clockwork. Warlords, paying off their soldiers in livers and kidneys and genitals, depopulate whole areas. Vast hospital cities cover the land from the air conditioned hospital palaces of the rich radiating out to field hospitals and open air operating booths. The poor are rising in huge mobs. They are attacking government warehouses where the precious parts are stored. Everyone who can afford it has dogs and guards to protect himself from roving bands of part hunters like the dreaded Wild Doctors who operate on each other after the battle, cutting the warm quivering parts from the dead and dying. Cut-and-grab men dart out of doorways and hack out a kidney with a few expert strokes of their four-inch scalpels. People have lost all shame. Here's a man who sold his daughter's last kidney to buy himself a new groin — appears on TV to appeal for funds to buy little Sally an artificial kidney and give her this last Christmas. On his arm is a curvaceous blonde known apparently as Bubbles. She calls him Long John, now isn't that cute?

A flourishing black market in parts grows up in the gutted

cities devastated by part riots. In terrible slums, scenes from Breughel and Bosch are re-enacted . . . misshapen masses of rotten scar tissue crawling with maggots supported on crutches and canes, in wheel-chairs and carts . . . Brutal as butchers, practitioners operate without anaesthetic in open air booths surrounded by their bloody knives and saws . . . the poor wait in part lines for diseased genitals, a cancerous lung, a cirrhotic liver. They crawl towards the operating booths holding forth nameless things in bottles — that they think are usable parts. Shameless swindlers who buy up operating garbage in job lots prey on the unwary.

And here is Mr Rich Parts. He is three hundred years old. He is still subject to accidental death, and the mere thought of it throws him into paroxysms of idiot terror. For days he cowers in his bunker, two hundred feet down in solid rock, food for fifty years. A trip from one city to another requires months of shifting and checking computerized plans and alternate routes to avoid the possibility of an accident. His idiotic cowardice knows no bounds. There he sits, looking like a Chimu vase with a thick layer of smooth purple scar tissue. Encased in this armor, his movements are slow and hydraulic. It takes him ten minutes to sit down. This layer gets thicker and thicker right down to the bone — the doctors have to operate with power tools. So we leave Mr Rich Parts, and the picturesque parts people, their monument a mountain of scar tissue.

Mr Hubbard said: 'The rightest right a man could be would be to live infinitely wrong.' I wrote 'wrong' for 'long' and the slip is significant — for the means by which immortality is realized in science fiction, which will soon be science fact, are indeed infinitely wrong, the wrongest wrong a man can be, vampiric or worse.

Improved transplant techniques open the question as to whether the ego itself could be transplanted from one body to another. And the further question as to exactly where this entity resides. Here is Mr Hart a trillionaire dedicated to his personal immortality. Where is this thing called Mr Hart? Precisely where, in the human nervous system, does this ugly death sucking, death dealing, death fearing *thing* reside . . . ? Science can give a tentative answer: the 'ego' seems to be located in the mid-brain at the top of the head. Well he thinks couldn't we just scoop it out of a healthy youth, throw his in the garbage where it belongs, and slide in MEEEEEEE. So he starts looking for a brain surgeon, a 'scrambled egg' man, and he wants the best.

128

When it comes to a short order job old Doc Zeit is tops. He can switch eggs in an alley . . .

Mr Hart embodies the competitive, acquisitive, success minded spirit that formulated American capitalism. The logical extension of this ugly spirit is criminal. Success is its own justification. He who succeeds deserves to succeed he is RIGHT. The operation is a success. The doctors have discreetly withdrawn. When a man wakes up in a beautiful new Bod, he can flip out. It wouldn't pay to be a witness. Mr Hart stands up and stretches luxuriously in his new body. He runs his hands over the lean young muscle where his pot belly used to be. All that remains of the donor is a blob of gray matter in a dish. Mr Hart puts his hands on his hips and leans over the blob.

'And how wrong can *you* be? DEAD.'

He spits on it and he spits ugly.

The final convulsions of a universe based on quantitative factors like money, junk and time, would seem to be at hand . . . The time approaches when no amount of money will buy anything and time itself will run out. In *The Methuselah Enzyme* by Fred Mustard Stewart, Dr Mentius, a Swiss scientist, has found the youth enzyme, which he calls Mentase. As it turns out, Tithy, for Tithonus, or Sauve, for *sauve qui peut*, would have been more apt. Young kids secrete this elixir and senior citizens need it special. Mentase is gradually phased out of the body from about the age of 25 to 60. The keyword is extraction. Mentius is a long way from the synthesis of Mentase but to use an untested substance extracted without their knowledge or consent from young people on old people? He feels a distinct twinge in his medical ethics. But Mentase he says grimly must not be lost to humanity. Mentius is regarded as a brilliant lunatic by his medical colleagues: where can he turn for funds? He takes on four rich clients who will bring the young donors . . .

'He must have blacked out in the immersion tank, Bill reflects. Later he found a tiny sticking plaster up near the hair line . . .' The kids don't know they are giving their Mentase to the elderly sponsor and here is one old creep who brings his own adolescent son to the clinic and sucks all the youth and goodness out of him. So the oldsters are getting younger and the kids . . .

'Hugh dear those interesting freckles . . . What are they?'

They're liver spots. The doctor has to admit he has made a real *dummheit* all around. The old farts don't produce any Mentase of their own all they have is what the doctor gives them. And now an emergency, a shocking emergency, quite unlooked for has arisen. The doctor reels ashen faced from his microscope. He knows that if the injections of Mentase are cut off the aging process will recommence at a vastly accelerated rate. The stricken senior citizen would age before one's eyes. 'While still alive, and aware of what was happening, you quite literally disintegrate,' he tells them flatly. 'The only relief you could possibly have would be to go insane.'

And the good doctor has some news for the kids who are already comparing liver spots.

'By cutting off part of your pineal gland we seem to have uh *halted* your production of Mentase and the result is in plain English that you are aging a hundred times as fast as normal,' the doctor admits lamely.

Acute shortage of Mentase. The key word is Extraction. The aging kids, now as lost to shame as their elders, in fact rapidly becoming elders, that is to say coarse, ugly, and as shameless as they are disgusting, go out to recruit more kids for the Mentase . . . paid in Mentase, of course, and each recruit must in turn recruit more donors. Think how that could build up in five years bearing in mind the extremely short productive period of the donors.

Puts me in mind of the old fur farm swindle. You invest $500 and buy a pair of mink. The farm is usually in Canada which has always been a center for mail fraud. The farm will take care of your mink who will breed every six months producing a litter of eight or more mink who in turn will pair and breed at the age of six months. Get a paper and pencil . . . and that's not all . . . some of the mink will be *mutants* green and blue and albino, and sea shell pink or maybe you hit the jackpot with rainbow mink, $2000 a pelt. As you luxuriate in rack after rack of ankle-length mink coats a letter etched in black arrives from the farm: regret to inform you your two minks died of distemper.

The ravening Mentase addicts need more and more and more. Any purely quantitative factor is devalued in time. With junk money Mentase, it takes more and more to buy less and less. Maybe Mr Hart has a warehouse full of Mentase to obtain which he has depopulated a continent; it will run out in time. But long before it runs out he will have reached a point where no amount of Mentase he can inject into his aging carcass will halt the aging process.

Mentase is a parable of vampirism gone berserk. But all vampiric blueprints for immortality are wrong not only from the ethical standpoint. They are ultimately unworkable. In *Space Vampires* Colin Wilson speaks of benign vampires. Take a little, leave a little. But they always take more than they leave by the basic nature of the vampiric process of inconspicuous but inexorable consumption. The vampire converts quality, live blood, vitality, youth, talent into quantity food and time for himself. He perpetrates the most basic betrayal of the spirit, reducing all human dreams to his shit. And that's the wrongest wrong a man can be. And personal immortality in a physical body is impossible since a physical body exists in time and time is that which ends. When someone says he wants to live forever he forgets that forever is a time word . . . All three-dimensional immortality projects are to say the least ill-advised, since they immerse the aspirant always deeper into time.

The tiresome concept of personal immortality is predicated on the illusion of some unchangeable precious essence that is greedy old MEEEEEE forever. The Buddhists say there is no MEEEEEE no unchanging ego . . .

What we think of as our ego is a defensive reaction just as the symptoms of an illness . . . fever, swelling, sweating are the body's reaction to an invading organism, so our beloved ego, arising from the rotten weeds of lust and fear and anger, has no more continuity than a fever sweat. There is no ego only a shifting process unreal as the Cities of the Odor-Eaters that dissolve in rain. A moment's introspection will demonstrate that we are not the same as we were a year ago, a week ago. This opens many doors. Your spirit could reside in a number of bodies, not as some hideous parasite draining the host, but as a helpful little visitor 'Roger the Lodger . . . don't take up much room . . . show you a trick or two . . . never overstay my welcome.'

Some of the astronauts were peculiar people. I think it was Grissom who was killed in the capsule fire . . . well he always ate *two* meals. And Randolph Scott is described as being notably *well developed* and *heavily muscled* and here's a nice little visitor just for *you*

> Heavily muscled Randy Scott
> You're my favorite astronaut
> Hunky Scotty oh yohoooo
> I'm going to hitch a ride with you.

This happens all the time. You think of someone and you can hear their voice in your throat, feel their face in yours and their eyes looking out. You will notice that this happens more with some people than with others. And some are more there in voice. I have but to think of Felicity Mason, an English friend, and her clear clipped upper-class British accents fairly ring through the room. And Gregory Corso has a strong absent voice. Let's face it, you are other people and other people are you. Take 50 photos of the same person over an hour. Some of them will look so unlike the subject as to be unrecognizable. And some of them will look like some other person: 'Why he looks just like Khrushchev with one gold tooth peeking out.'

The illusion of a separate inviolable identity limits your perceptions and confines you in time. You live in other people and other people live in you; 'visiting' we call it and of course it's ever so much easier with one's Clonies. When I first heard about cloning, I thought what a *fruitful* concept, why one could be in a hundred different places at once and *experience* everything the other clones did. I am amazed at the outcry against this good thing not only from Men of the Cloth but from scientists . . . the very scientists whose patient research has brought cloning within our grasp. The very thought of a clone disturbs these learned gentlemen. Like cattle on the verge of stampede they paw the ground mooing apprehensively . . . 'Selfness is an essential fact of life. The thought of human non-selfness is terrifying.'

Terrifying to *whom*? Speak for yourself you timorous old beastie cowering in your eternal lavatory. Too many scientists seem to be ignorant of the most rudimentary spiritual concepts. And they tend to be suspicious, bristly, paranoid-type people with huge egos they push around like some elephantiasis victim with his distended testicles in a wheelbarrow terrified no doubt that some skulking ingrate of a clone student will sneak into his very brain and steal his genius work. The unfairness of it brings tears to his eyes as he peers anxiously through his bifocals. He is reading a book *In His Image* by David Rorvick. In this book a rich old eccentric wants to get himself cloned and contacts the author who, being a scientific reporter, knows all the far-out researchers. In fact he knows just the doctor for the job who is named Darwin. But before he fixes Max up with Darwin, Max has to promise to be *ethical* about the whole thing. Absolutely only one clone at a time. Max must swear to abstain from any clonish act that could be construed as a take-over by cold-eyed *inhuman* clone armies.

A group of identical youths stand on a rocky point

overlooking a valley. One farts. No one smiles or alters his expression. One points. In a blur of movement all in perfect synch they gather their packs and rifles and move out.

A close-up as they move down a mountain trail shows that something is lacking in these faces, something that we are accustomed to see. The absence is as jarring as if the faces lacked a mouth or a nose. There is no face prepared to meet the faces that it meets, no self-image, no need to impress or assert. They blend into the landscape like picture-puzzle faces.

In the book Max refrains and settles down to watch his little clone grow. In my fictional extension he is more venturesome.

At this point I was engaged in another assignment which took me away for a year. When I returned, Roberto the chauffeur met me at the airport with new clothes and an expensive wrist watch. As we drove towards the hospital I saw that the Faculty was now an impressive complex of buildings. When we reached the Expanded Facility he led me into a lounge where I observed about fifty boys engaged in theatricals. Some were in clerical garb intoning 'Interfering with the designs of the Creator.' 'Each of us has a right to a special yet unique relation with the Creator . . .'

Others were up as doddering scientists meandering in senile dementia. 'We cannot ethically get to know if cloning is feasible.' 'Precipitating an identity crisis.'

A hideous scientist croaks out like some misshapen toad. 'Differences of appearance reinforce our sense of self and hence lend support to the feeling of *individual* worth we seek in ourselves and others.'

'The thought of human non-selfness is terrifying!' screeches a snippy old savant. He ducks into his study and recoils in horror. A replica of himself is sitting at his desk going through his notes. I realize that the boys are mocking the opponents of cloning. At this point Max comes in with Doctor Darwin. Darwin is a changed man. Gone are his petulance and hesitation, his prickly ego. He glows with health and confidence. The boys greet him boisterously.

'How many you kill today Doc?'

Max seizes both my hands and looks deep into my eyes with a quiet intense charm.

'Good to see you.'

The boys have stripped off their make-up and they are all perfect specimens of young manhood.

'Boys,' Max announces like a circus barker. 'The *Immaculate*, the *Virgin* birth is at hand.'

He leads the way to a maternity clinic got up as a manger where fifty girls are in labor. I notice they were wearing decompression suits . . .

'We got it down to a few minutes now,' Darwin tells me. 'They *pop* out . . .'

Even as he spoke there was a popping sound like the withdrawal of a viscous cork and a medic held up a squalling baby.

'Yipppeeeee!' a boy screamed. '*I'm cloned!*'

I pointed out to Max that all this was in flat violation of our agreement.

He doesn't hear me. 'All the resources of Trak are now channeled into clone factories . . . All over the world they are popping out . . . My little poppies I call them . . .'

Roberto does a chick breaking out of the shell act as he sings in hideous falsetto:

'PIO PIO PIO YO SOY UN POLLITO!'

And Max bellows with laughter. 'No I am not mad. Nor is this ego gone berserk. On the contrary, cloning is the end of the ego. For the first time the spirit of man will be able to separate itself from the human machine, to see it and use it as a machine. He is no longer identified with one special Me Machine. The human organism has become an artifact he can use like a plane or a space capsule.'

John Giorno wondered if maybe a clone of a clone of a clone would just phase out into white noise like copies of copies of a tape. As Count Korzybski used to say:

'I don't know, let's see.'

I postulate that true immortality can only be found in space. Space exploration is the only goal worth striving for. Over the hills and far away. You will know your enemies by those who attempt to block your path. Vampiric monopolists would keep you in time like their cattle.

'It's a good thing cows don't fly,' they say with an evil chuckle. The evil intelligent Slave Gods.

The gullible confused and stupid pose an equal threat owing to the obstructive potential of their vast numbers.

I have an interesting slip in my scrap book. News clipping from *The Boulder Camera*. Picture of an old woman with a death's head false teeth smile. She is speaking for the Women's Christian Temperance Union.

'WE OPPOSE CHILD ABUSE, INTEMPERANCE AND IMMORTALITY.'

The way to immortality is in space and Christianity is buried under slag heaps of dead dogma, sniveling prayers and empty promises *must* oppose immortality in space as the counterfeit always fears and hates the real thing. Resurgent Islam . . . born-again Christians . . . creeds outworn . . . excess baggage . . . *raus mit*!

Immortality is prolonged future and the future of any artifact lies in the direction of increased flexibility, capacity for change and ultimately mutation. Immortality may be seen as a by-product of function: 'to *shine* in use.' Mutation involves changes that are literally unimaginable from the perspective of the future mutant. Cold-blooded, non-dreaming creatures living in the comparatively weightless medium of water, could not conceive of breathing air, dreaming and experiencing the force of gravity as a basic fact of life. There will be new fears like the fear of falling, new pleasures and new necessities. There are distinct advantages to living in a supportive medium like water. Mutation is not a matter of logical choices.

The human mutants must take a step into the unknown, a step that no human being has ever taken before.

'We were the first that ever burst into that silent sea.'

'We are such stuff as dreams are made of.'

Recent dream research has turned up a wealth of data but no one has assembled the pieces into a workable field theory.

By far the most significant discovery to emerge from precise dream research with volunteer subjects is the fact that *dreams are a biological necessity* for all warm-blooded animals. Deprived from REM sleep, they show all the symptoms of sleeplessness no matter how much dreamless sleep they are allowed. Continued deprivation would result in death.

All dreams in male subjects except nightmares are accompanied by erection. No one has proffered an explanation. It is interesting to note that a male chimpanzee who did finger and dab paintings, and was quite good too, went into a sexual frenzy during his creative acts.

Cold-blooded animals do not dream. All warm-blooded creatures including birds do dream.

John Dunne discovered that dreams contain references to future time as experienced by the dreamer. He published his findings *An Experiment With Time* in 1924. Dream references, he points out, relate not to the event itself but to *the time when the subject learns of the event*. The dream refers to the future of the dreamer. He says that anybody who will write his dreams down over a period of time will turn up precognitive references. *Dreams involve time travel.* Does it follow then that time travel is a necessity?

I quote from an article summarizing the discoveries of Professor Michel Jouvet. Jouvet, using rapid eye movement techniques, has been able to detect dreaming in animals in the womb even in developing birds in the egg. He found that animals like calves and foals, who can fend for themselves immediately after birth, dream a lot in the womb and relatively little after that. Humans and kittens dream less in the womb and are unable to fend for themselves at birth.

He concluded that human babies could not walk or feed themselves until they had *enough practice in dreams.* This indicates that the function of dreams is to *train the being for future conditions.* I postulate that the human artifact is biologically designed for space travel. So human dreams can be seen as *training for space conditions.* Deprived of this vital link with our future in space, with no reason for living, we die.

Art serves the same function as dreams. Plato's *Republic* is a blueprint for a death camp. An alien invader, or a domestic elite, bent on conquest and extermination, could rapidly immobilize the earth by cutting dream lines, just the way we took care of the Indians. I quote from *Black Elk Speaks* by John Neihardt (Pocket Books):

'The nation's hoop is broken and scattered like a ring of smoke. There is no center any more. The sacred tree is dead and all its birds are gone.'

It Is Necessary to Travel . . .

'It is necessary to travel. It is not necessary to live.' These words inspired early investigators when the vast frontier of unknown seas opened to their sails in the fifteenth century. Space is the new frontier. Is this frontier open to youth? I quote from the London *Daily Express*, December 30, 1968: 'If you are a fit young man under twenty-five with lightning reflexes who fears nothing in heaven or on earth and has a keen appetite for adventure don't bother to apply for the job of astronaut.' They want 'cool dads' trailing wires to the 'better half' from an aqualung. Dr Paine of the Space Center in Houston says: 'This flight was a triumph for the squares of this world who aren't ashamed to say a prayer now and then.' Is this the great adventure of space? Are these men going to take the step into regions literally unthinkable in verbal terms? To travel in space you must leave the old verbal garbage behind: God talk, country talk, mother talk, love talk, party talk. You must learn to exist with no religion, no country, no allies. You must learn to live it alone in silence. Anyone who prays in space is not there.

The last frontier is being closed to youth. However there are many roads to space. To achieve complete freedom from past conditioning is to be in space. Techniques exist for achieving such freedom. These techniques are being concealed and withheld. We must search for and consider techniques for discovery.

The Four Horsemen of the Apocalypse

Famine... Plague... War... Death... Portentous and purposeful as the Priest advancing on a dying man to administer the last rites ... so the four caballeros, by their solid presence, indicate that time has been called for that particular biological or sociological experiment... Closing time gentlemen.

Dinosaurs bellow piteously. Famine saddles up his cayoose and gallops through lush swampland leaving dust bowls behind him. The outmoded dinosaurs subside into museum skeletons, gaped at by human spectators. Their day will come... The CIA and other organizational dinosaurs bellow piteously... We were just doing our job ... trouble deep heaven with their bootless cries.

At the present time the situation is more complicated, since the subject of this experiment, in this case the human species, can to some extent control the conditions of the experiment. Not such an advantage as one would think since they cannot control themselves. Since the human creature has demonstrated through the centuries a stubborn disclination to control himself... However, not so ... If I may indulge a whimsy, had we been dinosaurs we might have built great dams to preserve our simple way of life, and hunted down the despicable mammals as the egg-sucking rats they were. (Some have theorized that the mammals undermined the dinosaurs by eating their eggs.)

There is such basic disagreement as to how existing conditions can be altered, by exactly who and for the benefit of whom these wondrous laterations should be made. That stupidity and shortsighted self-interest may well swamp spacecraft earth before the horsemen can saddle up. Meanwhile the spectral riders are being eagerly wooed by the CIA and similar agencies in other countries. Wise and far-sighted men who will no doubt use their awesome knowledge of famine, war, plague and death for the good of all mankind...

'Put that joker Death on the line. Take care of Mao and his gang of cutthroats.'

Famine, seemingly the most fortuitous of the quartet, is transcending the caprices of weather, deforestation, and over-population, and catching a new look. We can extend the area of famine to include the lack of substance or condition essential to the support of life. We can in fact create needs quite as compelling as the need for food or water. Drug addiction is an example of a biologic need artificially produced by the administration of opiates. No doubt drugs much more habit forming than heroin could be produced in the laboratory by tinkering with the habit-forming molecule . . . We now have substance X which can be introduced into the water supply, food or even in a gaseous form into enemy air. X has no effects unless it is removed . . . then a battery of crippling symptoms, disabling symptoms reduce the enemy to impotence. Think of it . . . The Russkies at our mercy and they don't even know it yet.

There are certain metabolic illnesses like Wilson's disease in which the subject is unable to absorb certain essential vitamins and minerals no matter how much he ingests . . . In fact it is not too far-fetched to conceive of inducing metabolic changes that would reduce the absorption of any nutrients so that no matter how much he eats the subject will die of starvation . . .

The alliance between war and plague was cemented with the first germ warfare experiments. In this area there have been a number of interesting developments despite some mealy mouthed talk about discontinuing such experiments and the closing down of the biological and chemical warfare center at Fort Detrick in Maryland. The center is now dedicated to cancer research. (Cancer research incidently overlaps the more sophisticated areas of biologic weaponry.) As early as World War II England had the doomsday bug which was a mutated virus produced by exposing such viruses as hepatitis and rabies to radiation . . . A number of experiments have been carried out.

It is difficult to believe that such a promising line of research was abandoned, and disturbing to speculate or contemplate where this research is at the present time. There has been talk of discontinuing such experiments. Here is an item from the London *Times* of 18 April 1971 . . . New Cancer Virus made by accident . . . A completely new Virus probably capable of producing cancer in humans has been made by accident in an American research laboratory . . . fears expressed by cautious scientist that some medical research could inadvertently produce new forms of human disease instead of curing existing ones . . . The new agent was discovered by Dr Aronson of the National Cancer Institute near Washington . . . under special conditions the mouse virus could be persuaded to infect human cancer cells grown in a test tube. Though the process was an extremely inefficient one . . . Dr Abrahams now reports in Nature that the mouse virus has changed its nature . . . it has become highly infective to human cells and completely non-infective to mouse cells . . . a permanent major genetic change has occurred in the virus . . . what amounts to a completely new virus has emerged. The virus has picked up a human gene and incorporated it giving it the ability to multiply readily in human cells . . . Sir Macfarlane Burnet warns in the *Lancet* . . . of the almost unimaginable catastrophe of a virgin soil epidemic involving all the populated regions of the world.

And the age-old dream of a selective pestilence is now within the reach of modern technology . . . London *Times* . . .

Ethnic weapons that could wipe out one race and leave another unharmed could soon be developed. A leading geneticist Carl Larson said icily: 'Ethnic weapons would employ differences in human genetic configuration to make genetic variations to make genocide particularly attractive as a form of war.' Writing in the US Army Military Review Larson argues enzyme levels can vary according to race . . . The absence of certain enzymes can cause death. Enzyme deficiencies could be exploited by chemical warfare. 'It will probably be possible to develop a chemical which will act as an enzyme inhibitor . . . Say you find an enzyme inhibitor to which ninety percent of all Europeans would be vulnerable which effects only ten percent of Africans . . . Since the inhibitor could tell friend from foe, no matter how intermingled it is, it would be the superselective military weapon, that all military thinkers dream of. Larson admitted more genetic research is needed before ethnic weapons become a practical reality.'

Well that item is over ten years old . . . Selection could be carried much further even to the point of annihilation that effects only people with certain traits of character, since character traits indicate metabolic variations. If anyone is habitually angry and antagonistic this effects his entire metabolism. The study of psychosomatic medicine has repeatedly shown that patients with certain character traits are more subject to certain illnesses.

It seems then that War, Plague and Famine are merging.

What about the last horseman: Death? Can death maintain a separation from the means by which death is produced? From the horsemen who do the job? Or is the union between death and the instructions of death about to be consummated? . . . There are those who think so.

Psychosomatic medicine has demonstrated that patients with certain character structures are more disposed to certain illness. We can go further: characterological and metabolic alteration can be induced by environmental pressures. It is not difficult to pressure large numbers of potential or actual enemies towards a way of life that will bring them within the range of our biological agent. Forced urbanization was the CIA policy in Vietnam that was implemented by Bill Colby, concentrating population in urban centers. Diet and the whole psychological and physical environment underwent specific alterations. And the disease agent is provided with receptive hosts in convenient proximity.

The *Herald Tribune*, June 1970: 'The Synthetic Gene Revolution.' Dr Har Khorana at the University of Wisconsin has created an artificial gene. News that may rank with the splitting of the atom as a milestone in our control — or is it lack of control? — of the physical universe . . .

'It is the beginning of the end.' This was the reaction to the news from the science attaché at one of Washington's major embassies. 'If you can make genes, you can eventually make new viruses, for which there is no cure. Any little country with a good biochemist could make such biological weapons. It would take only a small laboratory. If it can be done, someone will do it. To be sure it is almost science fiction. Unfortunately science fiction has a bad habit of coming true.'

The virus for which there is no cure could be death itself. The genetic message of Death . . .

The gentlemen riders have no meaning outside a human context; they are in fact human inventions. So let us examine the human context. The first thing that would impress a visitor from outer space is the tremendous inexplicable gap between potential and performance. No species that isn't fundamentally flawed could be this stupid this consistently. Consider the human organism as an artifact. Comparative evaluation will show us where this artifact is, what is wrong with it, and how far it has to go. Look at the first powered planes, and compare with a modern transport or fighter plane. Even if we were transported back to 1910 we could still see that this artifact is in

141

a rudimentary stage. Riddled with flaws, it must improve or disappear.

Death is that which, when it occupies you, you are dead. Death is eviction from the earth body. Death is an unbearable presence. People die to avoid it . . . Death can be simply defined as what kills you . . . We all have a photographic memory of the past . . . This has been recovered under hypnosis and with the increased use of tape recorders there are more and more cross checks on the accuracy of the materials recovered. And messages purporting to come from some dead VIP through a medium could be checked for voice prints. Quite as definitive as finger prints for purposes of identification. Do we have on some deep biological level a memory of the future as well? Do we all know when and how we will die? A disquieting thought and even more disquieting could be a virus or a microwave that releases the death message to zero in on Death, directed by some molecular affinity to release your death instructions. The virus or wave simply gets keys in the latent death message. It is interesting that knowledge of such breath-taking implications may be buried in Top Secret Files. If we have a virus with an affinity for death, it might just be a good place to start looking for our ancient antagonist, Death itself. Some ocultists say the death center is located in the back of the neck. Perhaps we would become a bit more precise about the exact meaning of this death center. Is this where our final instructions, the last telegrams are written out and the death warrant officially signed? Interesting questions . . . And I fear they are beyond the scope of those who think of death as a company cop.

The most crassly utilitarian research may turn up the most spectacular theoretical conclusions and applications in other areas.

I am not concerned here with the history of germ warfare but with the outer frontiers of biological and chemical weaponry at the present time.

The processes set in inexorable motion by the industrial revolution with its total commitment to quantity and quantitave criterion, are just beginning to reveal themselves as the death trap they always were. At a time when the hope of the human race lies in space exploration and above all in biological mutation, we are threatened by a Moron Majority committed to enforcing their stupid bestial, bigoted opinions on everybody else. To such people the very thought of mutation is the ultimate sacrifice. These are the guard dogs that will keep the human race in neoteny until this experiment is quietly buried . . . until it disappears. That is what we are facing here. An extermination program. All the basic moves thought out in the turn of the century. Topheavy urban populations that depend for their existence on the industrial machine continuing to function on the vast unseen bureaucracy that provides food and services. What form could rebellion take if the communists took over the country they would either have to keep the present bureaucracy in place or provide a new one to fill exactly the same functions. All paths are blocked by numbers, by more and more of what we have too much of already. This means that the human stock, the human product, far from reaching a point where it could be possible to fulfill our destiny in space is inevitably declining and devalued just as the currency is devalued. Like the army — more and more to buy less and less. What we are dealing with is the virus mechanism of replication. The human products that best lend themselves to replication have a higher potential for survival in a deadly environment. That assures the survival of the species. Jerry Falwell and his Moral Majority being a case in point: a majority that prides itself on its unthinking adherence to certain rigid standards that have nothing to do with the survival of the species. This product produces and consumes. The full force of mass production capitalism is behind it like a vast reservoir . . . It votes. It is tirelessly devoted to promulgating its image and forcing that image on everyone else. Now faced by this deadly process the history of our pianet is a history of idiocy highlighted by a few morons who stand out as comparative geniuses. Today no supergenius has achieved what might be called normal intelligence in terms of the potential functioning of the human artifact.

We see now that the gentlemen riders are eliminating each other. Famine is after all very old hat and very slow, but the chief of the Death Division has some explicit ideas . . . He has that awful shy and cute duck manner . . . 'Well you see we've been you might say streamlining the department to uh consider famine in the very widest sense of the word . . . death deficiency . . . This of course can be a lack of some basic atmospheric necessity such as oxygen . . .' The press start to gag and show signs of asphyxia . . . The chief turns a button '. . . and so you see it can also refer to what we might call spiritual famine. Faced by a prospect of Levittown houses built to the sky the target collapses and dies for the simple lack of any reason not to. No do not underestimate us, gentlemen . . . Are you bored with breathing? An air famine would amuse you? I think not really . . . But of course we're taking war out of that horrible nuclear thing so bad for *our* image, my dear so its simply Plague and death getting together, famine and war standing by.'

The Great Glut

Many ecologists, including Allen Ginsberg, have questioned the long-range wisdom of dumping sewage into our lakes and rivers and seas, killing the fish or rendering them unfit for our ever-growing consumption. Cousteau sounded a word of warning: 'The seas are already forty percent dead.' Allen suggests that we simply reverse directions and channel our shit back to the soil.

Now to put this fruitful concept into operation. All the toilets of New York City empty into vats where the rich substance is reduced to liquid form and piped into relays of tanker trucks to be conveyed to the hinterlands, where the eager farmer waits. Every block has a dog shitting area to facilitate the collection of dog shit which would otherwise foul the barren pavements and asphalt. All recyclable garbage is collected and poured into the vats. Patriotic Boy Scouts organize vast shit hikes to fertilize the truck farms surrounding the cities.

A further step is obvious. The human body makes the best fertilizer that can be got. So corpses are collected and fed into the vats to be processed with the shit and garbage and returned to the soil. Posters throughout the city admonish the citizen: 'GIVE IT BACK TO MOTHER EARTH.' Stern-faced farmers point to the passerby: 'WE NEED YOU.' Soon a funeral is an ecological outrage as unpopular as a fur coat. The hinterland achieves a fertility unknown in the history of mankind. Vast vegetables pile up in the markets — potatoes as big as watermelons, carrots six feet long, artichokes the size of washtubs. And the hogs fed on the soft mushy corn reach a weight of two tons, wallowing in their shit, too fat to move. You can cut the soft lardy flesh with a fork.

In fact all this food still smells of the shit and corpses it is made of, as if the glutted land cannot transmute the superabundance of nutrients which seep into the vegetables and the hogs, the chickens big as ostriches, the rhinoceros-size steers. The people fed on this food are bloated and stink of carrion and sewage, belching coal gas. Many of them are confined by their weight to hydraulic wheelchairs, with receptacles for shit which are emptied into containers provided on every block like mail boxes.

The cities are dying of surfeit. Some of the young people refuse to eat the disgusting vegetables swollen with loathsome ichors and the soft greasy stinking meat, which they execrate as 'fit only for the consumption of underprivileged vultures.' They take refuge in remote barren regions where the soil is too poor to qualify for the bounteous urban overflow. Monstrous plant forms evolve in the plains of Kansas, Iowa, Illinois, Oklahoma and Texas, man-eating plants fed on rendered corpse juice, to be in turn ploughed under by combines of tractors manned by farmers in gas masks. The end product is an unpopulated jungle; primeval swamps, vines and firs slowly grow over the dying cities. Only the sparse populations of the poor soil areas survive the Great Glut, which subsides over the years into virgin forest and untouched jungles of teeming fertility swarming with animal and insect and vegetable life. Ecology has won by a glut.

POP and the Heroids

I mentioned recently a super painkiller now under development: P.O.P., Pituitary Opioid Peptide. POP. This morphine-like substance extracted from the pituitary glands of cattle is fifty times stronger than morphine as a painkiller, and non-habit-forming. You see the implications: Non-habit-forming, no side effects like constipation and loss of sexual energy, and fifty times the strength of morphine, twenty-five times that of heroin. So why should anyone ever have to say 'I'm hurting'?

The medical profession tried desperately to throw a block in and keep it on prescription, but mobs poured out of the ghettoes and the suburbs screaming 'Death to the RX profiteers!' I figured to get in on the ground floor of this good thing.

You can see the complete obliteration of the whole Protestant ethic: 'You gotta pay for pleasure with suffering.' But here it was in a syringe, one pop lasts a week. And think of all the subliminal pain we carry about all the time, not only physical but psychic: the fear, the depression, the boredom and dreariness, all gone, just like that — POP!

Now fear needs a reservoir of pain to draw on, and that reservoir is suddenly cut. No one needs to drink or smoke any more, they don't have anything they need to forget about or escape from . . . POP . . . Gotta be a catch somewhere. But is there a catch? The usage of this divine substance would allow for a much more modest living standard. When you are feeling no pain you don't need cars and TVs and luxurious overheated quarters. A bare cubicle and the simplest food will suffice. The whole human equation of pleasure and pain, the struggle to achieve pleasure or at least comfort and the even stronger necessity of avoiding pain and discomfort, has been rendered obsolete. War and crime disappear. Why fight when you have it made? Why steal when your needs are so simple and easily satisfied? Pop will take care of you. Pop will cover you in a warm blanket. Pop will supply all your needs. End of the human rat race — POP.

If you find it — as I do — difficult to conceive of a painkilling drug that is not habit-forming, here is another script:

'Well, Doctor?' asked a highly-placed narcotics official.

'The drug is not heroin. It's an organic compound with a gold base. Probably synthesized from a drug similar to *bannisteria caapi*.'

'One of the psychedelics?'

'Undoubtedly it has psychedelic properties. At the same time it is a cell-blanketing agent, like morphine and heroin, but much more potent. To put it simply for a layman, its psychedelic properties expose more area to blanket.'

'It is a habit-forming drug?'

'It is indeed. Thirty times more habit-forming than heroin, and in consequence the withdrawal symptoms are proportionately more drastic. Animals given *one* injection of this drug die in convulsions if the drug is withheld beyond eight hours even though industrial doses of heroin are administered. Capture for such an addict means death in literally inconceivable agony, since the drug is an inconceivable painkiller. It is also a *retroactive* painkiller, wiping out all past reservoirs of pain and consequently fear as well. These Heroids have only one fear: withdrawal. Owing to the drug's psychedelic properties, the addicts are in telepathic communication. They go armed at all times. The Heroids will not be taken alive.'

'But who is distributing this hellish stuff?'

'That's your department. My guess is it leaked from some top secret project — whether American, Russian, Chinese or French does not matter at this point. Point is, these addicts have a vital necessity to communicate their addiction as a matter of survival. Remember that only one exposure establishes lifelong addiction. They could put it in milk, soft drinks, candy bars, or addict whole populations with aerosol bombs.'

'My God.' The high narc steps to a window. He needs a breath of fresh air. 'Of course it's the Commies' he thinks. 'The *fiends* . . .' He flushes with rage. Then he feels a little stab of pain and looks down to see a dart embedded in his stomach. It must have come from across the street. His flush fades to a gray-green pallor as a cool blue frequency fixes him right to metal. Feels so good that feeling, he could just swim in it forever and ever. And a little cold voice in his brain is telling him what to do. He turns towards the doctor, the dart concealed in his hand, and jabs the dart into the doctor's arms. The doctor smiles.

'That wasn't necessary, except as a demonstration of your loyalty to our cause. You see, I became addicted during my analysis of the drug. I think we are now ready for that emergency meeting with the President and all the top brass. If you want something done, go right to the top. Within an hour, Air Force planes will blanket America with aerosol bombs. Then these States will be truly united.

'This drug is only the beginning. Soon we will have drugs a hundred, *two* hundred times stronger than heroin. First America, then the world . . . a world without pain and without fear, working shoulder to shoulder to produce the perfect product.'

Mind War

Earlier I have suggested that the CIA, the Russians, and the Chinese have all set up top secret centers to study and apply psychic techniques to political ends. Those of you who have read *Psychic Discoveries Behind the Iron Curtain* will infer that the Russians are ahead of us.

Now anyone who has lived for any time in countries like Morocco where magic is widely practiced has probably seen a curse work. I have. However, curses tend to be hit or miss, depending on the skill and power of the operator and the susceptibility of a victim. And that isn't good enough for the CIA or any similar organization: 'Bring us the ones that work not sometimes but *every* time.' So what is the logical forward step? To devise machines that can concentrate and direct psychic force with predictable effects. I suggest that what the CIA is, or was working on, at their top secret Nevada installation may be described as *computerized* black magic. If Curse A doesn't make it, Curse Program B automatically goes into operation — and so on.

I recommend to your attention a book called *The Mind Masters* by John Rossmann. This is ostensibly a fanastic science fiction novel, interesting more for its content than its style, that may well contain some real inside information. The story concerns a researcher who has been disillusioned by his work on Project Pandora, an American psychic training center run by a Colonel Pickett, who is strongly reminiscent of the mad General Ripper in Doctor Strangelove, right down to the cigar. Only he is unloosing *psychic* warfare rather than nuclear bombs, having convinced himself that this form of warfare is more effective and more easily controlled for elitist objectives. The disillusioned researcher, one Britt St. Vincent, is contacted by Mero, a private institute dedicated to opposing these black magic centers. (It should be obvious that only *black* magic has 'military applications.')

After he has been taken to Mero's secret headquarters, Britt is briefed by Dr Webster on the purposes of Mero. Dr Webster cites an early report by columnist Jack Anderson that the reason the Johnson-Kosygin summit conference in 1967 at Glassboro, New Jersey, was held in such a remote spot was that this was the world's first summit conference on *psychic warfare*. He recalls for Britt how the CIA, while making an electronic sweep of the U.S. Embassy in Moscow for listening devices, discovered some very unusual electromagnetic emanations pulsing through the building. (Later it came out that the Soviets had stepped up the power to a point where Embassy officials and their families were in danger from the high-voltage microwave radiation, which can cause confusion, migraines, and even death.) Not long after, the CIA confirmed that this was in fact part of a much larger psychic attack on the Embassy. When the Defense Department launched its top-secret psychic counterattack, according to columnist Anderson, it was code-named Project Pandora.

Dr Webster goes on to tell Britt: 'Glassboro wasn't the end of it, Britt . . . obviously. By easily diverting funds within their mammoth defense budgets, small groups of supermilitarists here and in Russia covertly continued psychic programs . . .

The violent student rioting of the late Sixties was largely instigated by electronic mood-control devices that were derived from the psychic discoveries of Project Pandora. The riots, it is now evident, were the first phase of a massive plot. The students were used by U.S. military extremists for two purposes. First, the riots tended to discredit the student causes. Secondly, the civil disturbances conveniently provided the plotters with the necessary reasons to reinstate some of their psychic weapons programs under the guise of 'crowd control' research. Britt learns that similar secret psychic research is still advancing rapidly in China, France, Israel, Egypt, South Africa and Chile, in addition to the United States and Russia.

'Although these scattered groups are currently working to beat *each other* to the secret of powers that will give them world control, there is a good possibility that they could even now join forces and make a *combined* psychic bid for world control — and at this moment they appear to stand an almost even chance of succeeding if they joined forces.'

And what would the future look like if such groups actually exist and if they do combine and take over ? An elitist world state very much along the lines laid down by the Nazis. At the top would be a theocracy trained in psychic control techniques implemented by computerized electronic devices that would render opposition psychologically impossible. Entry to this privileged class would be permitted only to those whose dedication to the world state was absolute and unquestioning. In short, you don't get in by merit or ability but by being an all around one hundred percent shit. Under this ruling, elite of power addicts would consist of an anonymous service collective of functionaries, managers, and bureaucrats. And below them the slave workers.

There would be no place for dissent or independent research. The troublesome artist would be eliminated or absorbed. The elite lives happily ever after, at the top of a control state that makes 1984 seem cozy and nostalgic.

In the Interests of National Security

Frank Olsen, a civilian biochemist working on a top-secret project for the CIA, apparently committed suicide on Nov. 28th, 1953, by throwing himself through a tenth-floor window in the Statler-Hilton Hotel in New York City. Perhaps someone should have a look at the window in question. Throwing oneself through a window set in metal frames is quite a feat.

Colonel Ruwet, Olsen's boss in something called the Special Operations Division, was involved with a CIA contract so secret that members working on various aspects of it did not even discuss their work with each other. And what was this so secret project? Ruwet refuses to say. We know now that one thing they were working on was LSD or the more potent BZ in gaseous form. They wanted something that would incapacitate an enemy without doing any lasting harm. It's more humane that way you see. This laudable project could have been easily handled by any college chemistry major. LSD is effective in very small doses and it is simply a question of finding a suitable suspension medium. Such a gas was developed and subsequently used in Vietnam, with what results we have not been told. Why then such elaborate precautions to conceal the project from the Russian military, who were admittedly ahead of us in drug research at the time? Why should Ruwet cover up something that is now common knowledge? We cannot but conclude that other projects in 'behavior modification' lurk behind the LSD smokescreen.

The ultimate form of behavior modification is Electric Brain Stimulation. EBS was developed by Dr Delgado and is described in his book *Physical Control of the Mind.* Electrodes implanted in the brain are activated by radio control. In this way Delgado has stopped a charging bull in its tracks. He has forced human subjects to pick up articles against their will . . . 'Your electricity is stronger than my will, Doctor,' one subject admitted as he tried to keep his hands from carrying out the electronic order. Delgado has also induced in human subjects fear, rage, sexual excitement, and euphoria, all at push-button

153

control. A thing like that could solve a lot of problems. The only limitation is the necessity of implanting electrodes in the brain of the subject. Can this limitation be overcome to achieve the same results without electrodes? EBS simply delivers a small electric current to certain brain areas. The brain itself emits small electric currents and there is no doubt that obsessive thoughts result from the auto-stimulation of certain brain areas. Could directed auto-stimulation be induced by the administration of a drug? Could a virus directed to certain brain areas serve as a terminal for electrical impulses delivered by radio control? If this was or is one of the secret projects Colonel Ruwet was engaged in, the need for secrecy is understandable, since such convenient modifications would be directed primarily against dissident elements within the United States.

Biological warfare has come a long way since 1953. Just how far it has come and how far it can go is leaking out from civilian projects. Here is a clipping from the Paris *Herald Tribune*: 'Beginning of the End — The Synthetic Gene Revolution . . . In a laboratory at 125 University Avenue, Madison, Wisconsin, a chemist from India, Dr Har Khorana, has made a gene. It is the first completely synthetic copy of one of the chemical molecules that direct life processes. "It is the beginning of the end." This was the immediate reaction to this news from the science attaché at one of Washington's major embassies. If you can make genes, he explained, you can eventually make new viruses for which there are no cures. "Any little country with good biochemists could make such biological weapons. It would take only a small laboratory. If it can be done, someone will do it."' And presumably any big country could do it quicker and better. Just as well to keep a thing like that under wraps, isn't it now?

And here's another from the London *Times*, 18 April 1971: 'New Cancer Virus Made By Accident . . . A completely new virus probably capable of causing cancer in humans has been made by accident in an American research laboratory. Its appearance is likely to reinforce fears already expressed by cautious scientists that some medical research could inadvertently produce new forms of human disease instead of curing existing ones. Sir Macfarlane Burnet, in a provocative article, bluntly warned: "Any escape into circulation that was not immediately dealt with could grow into the almost unimaginable catastrophe of a 'virgin soil' epidemic . . . involving all the populated regions of the world."'

154

And here's another: 'Genocide Made Easy ... Ethnic weapons that could wipe out one race and leave another unharmed could soon be developed. A leading Swedish geneticist, Carl Larson, says icily, "Ethnic weapons would employ differences in human genetic configuration to make genocide a particularly attractive form of war."' And Larson published his findings in the U.S. Army Military Review. It is the super-selective weapon that all military thinkers dream of. '"More genetic research is needed," he admitted, "but we should be thinking about this now if only to prevent such a weapon from being developed. We must not let it creep upon us unawares."'

Civilian researchers publish their findings. Top secret projects can then develop these findings in negative directions designated under 'military use,' but they do not publish *their* findings. They are withholding valuable knowledge not only from the public but from other workers in specialized fields. If we lived in the Middle Ages, the fact that the world is round would be a top secret enabling us to attack the enemy from the rear.

This is a game planet. All games are hostile and basically there is only one game, and that game is war. Research into altered states of consciousness — which might result in a viewpoint from which the game itself could be called into question — is inexorably drawn into the game. One of the rules of this game is that there cannot be final victory since that would mean the end of the war game. Every player must believe in final victory and endeavor to attain final victory with all his resources. In consequence all existing technologies are directed towards producing total weapons that could end the game by killing all players. Is there any way out of this impasse of national security at the expense of global insecurity? Certainly a prerequisite for any solution would be for all countries to put all their top secrets right on the table.

The only thing that could unite this planet is an all-out program for the exploration of space. As Brion Gysin says, we are here to go. If all nations saw the earth as a space station and landing field, the concept of war would be irrelevant. Is there any possibility of this happening? Not so long as those who make their living from the war game continue to control the resources of the planet and to direct all discoveries to military ends. So far the military and the CIA have managed to hide the full scope of secret operations by admitting what is already known . . . Army Admits Experiments with LSD Gas — big deal. The gas was used in Vietnam and the story came out in the Paris Herald Tribune six years ago. Army Tested Drug More Potent Than LSD — fifteen years ago I talked to a Dutch chemist who told me a drug had been developed so much more potent than LSD that they could not take the responsibility of administering it to human subjects, even with their full knowledge and consent, owing to the possibility of residual neural damage. In any case the drug had only been released to the military, who, it seems, did not hesitate to take the responsibility of administering the drug to human subjects without their knowledge *or* consent.

'We acted in the interests of national security.' they say smugly. It's the old war game, from here to eternity. Where would the military and the CIA be without it? It would seem that only a miracle could shock the planet into a realization that the game will kill us all unless we stop playing it.

Notes From Class Transcript*

I use scientific material in my fiction to get ideas for science, just to show the range and possibility of things that are actually going on. My use of building up identikit pictures is to get an idea of a character, maybe one I first encountered in a dream. I will find someone in reality that looks like that character and take a picture. I may find a picture in a magazine that resembles them. Or I may find a similar character in someone else's writing. In that way you slowly build up an identikit picture of your character.

I may have many sources for one character. All characters are composites. I think that's a mistake that writers often make when they start: they try to have just one real character. In other words, they are working from real characters and transcribing more or less directly. I mean literal transcription. Of course a writer's idea of a person is always a fiction in itself. Like Kerouac's picture of Neal Cassady. Well, I saw a very different Neal than the one he saw. You have *On the Road*, where Neal is always talking. Well, he had a great capacity for silence. I've driven with him for eight hours and he never said a thing.

In connection with schizophrenic writing, I've done a great deal of exploration in the direction of schizophrenic art, much of which is not very distinguished. But most of that was done by people who had some inclination towards painting, who might have been painters. So what I was interested in was writers who had the concept of schizophrenia. I knew one who was a poet; he was a great admirer of T. S. Eliot and his work was very much like Eliot's. You could say it's imitative of Eliot, but perhaps it's the opposite. That little trick that Eliot has, that stylistic trick, is noticeable in schizophrenic poetry, but unfortunately I don't have any of this poetry available. I just remember a few phrases like 'Doctorhood is being made with me,' or titles like *At Swim Two Birds* the same stylistic tricks of language that are found in Eliot and in the earlier poems of MacLeish.

You ask about the effects of grass on the creative mind.

* This is edited from answers to questions from students in class after a lecture.

157

Hallucinogenic drugs tend to reduce the necessity to dream. People will dream less if they are using grass or LSD or any of those drugs, because they are doing their dreaming in a waking state. By hallucinogenic I don't mean it produces actual hallucinations. It certainly extends awareness and I think makes your imagery more vivid, while at the same time you recognize it as imagery — you don't see it as an hallucination. As to the literature of the hallucinogenics, I don't think that such a literature exists. People are not going to become writers just because they are high. Undoubtedly a drug that increases awareness will give people ideas and imagery and so forth. But I don't think there is anything that we could call hashish writing, LSD writing, or mescaline writing. There is a lot of writing done by people after they have taken LSD; I remember whole collections of it. Most of it is terrible, vague, and in essence not good writing. But these people were not experienced writers.

Who Did What Where and When?

I have made several references to *Science and Sanity* by Count Korzybski. This book should be required reading for all college students and for anyone who is concerned with precision of thought and expression. Journalists and scientists especially. The Count points out that generalities without a clear referent are misleading and meaningless. 'Everyone knows that... Informed opinion indicates... Most people will agree...' What people will agree to what where and when? I have had reporters ask me whether I thought the American people were moving toward the right. What people? Farmers? Book-of-the-Month-Club ladies on the east coast? College students? Ghetto residents?

In His Image by David Rorvik contains a number of quotations from *scientists* who oppose cloning, and seem to be incapable of composing a semantically respectable statement.

'Selfness is an essential fact of life.'

To whom is it essential? Has no one told the learned gentleman that eastern spiritual disciplines with millions of followers are designed to eliminate the 'self'?

'The thought of human non-selfness is terrifying.' Whom does it terrify, Professor?

I do not argue with his viewpoint. If he chooses to treasure that querulous, frightened, defensive, petty, boring entity he calls his 'self' that is his affair. I am taking him to task on semantic grounds. He is talking nonsense.

'I consider selfness an essential fact of my life. The thought of human non-selfness terrifies me.'

Now it is a meaningful statement.

'Difference of appearance reinforces our sense of self and hence lends support to the feeling of individual worth we seek in ourselves and from others.'

Our sense of self? *We* seek? He has the stunning impertinence to speak for all mankind.

The Count points out that Aristotelian *either or* logic, setting up such polarities as intellect *or* emotion, reason *or* instinct, does not correspond to what we know about the physical universe and the human nervous system. He uses the phrase 'neuromuscular intention behavior' to describe the reactions of an organism as a whole in relation to its environment. Every action is *both* instinctive *and* intellectual, involving the entire body and nervous system. A man is hungry. The magic and almost meaningless word instinct has been invoked. But in his primitive instinctive search for food he may cross streets, take cabs, pay fares, read menus, all activities of the rational intellect. It seems obvious, but here is Michel Jouvet, a French scientist, formulating a theory that dreams are 'instinctive'.

Consider what would happen if instinctive and rational behavior were actually operating on *either or* basis.

The scene is the Rock Hotel in Gibraltar. The Professor lopes in like an animal sniffing for food. The waiter doesn't like his looks and decides to give him the treatment. Now the Professor sits down and orders in a voice without inflection or any emotional tone like a speaking computer. He orders two portions of very rare roast beef telling the waiter that his 'other half' will be along in a minute, and a bottle of red wine. He finishes a cross-word puzzle. At the sight of his food he emits a gutty whine of anticipation and his stomach rumbles like a vast kraken. He snatches the meat and licks the plate in such an offensive manner that nearby diners turn away and retch. He composes himself and looks at the bottle. It is white wine. He signals to the waiter.

'I ordered red wine. White wine taken with meat can cause serious gastric disturbances.'

'Look Mister I wrote the order down.'

The Professor's eyes light up inside and he bares his bloody canines. He slides out of his seat in a sinuous purposeful manner and seizes the waiter by the lapels.

'Bring me red wine you hairy-assed rock ape or I drink it from your throat.'

The waiter twists free and runs for his life. The Professor sits down and writes an important formula on a napkin.

Let's keep it together, Professor.

An Epitaph*

A victim is acted upon rather than acting. He is injured, ill, incarcerated, starving, or dead — that is, affected by other people or by circumstances or both. Some people are in the category of born victim; they may be born into hopeless poverty or with congential deformities. Others have the status of victim thrust upon them by seemingly random circumstances — accidents, earthquakes, fires, floods, epidemics. Some achieve the condition of victim; they are accident or misfortune prone.

The hard-core victim is one who achieves his condition. The Egyptian hieroglyph of a man splitting his own head is applicable here. Take Hemingway for example; a toilet fell on his head in Paris, he shot his own foot trying to kill a gaffed fish, he was injured in a series of plane and car crashes. Indeed, the list of such achievers is a long one, with artists, writers and performers prominently featured: F. Scott Fitzgerald, Malcolm Lowry, Baudelaire, Rimbaud, Modigliani, Van Gogh, Janis Joplin, James Dean, Isadora Duncan, and Jack and Bobby Kennedy. The chronic victim is in some cases seemingly endowed with negative telekinetic powers. (One man has been hit by lightning 11 times!) They are bad luck for themselves and anyone in their vicinity. Just walk down the street with one of these Jonahs and something bad will happen.

So, you may ask, isn't a victim datebook unlucky right there? On the contrary, I think such a book can enable us to profit by the errors and misfortunes of our predecessors, and avoid some deadly snare. We are able to see what they could not, and take evasive action in time.

This is the principle of *minimax*: assume that the worst may happen and act accordingly; remember that lightning always strikes twice in the same place. This is a basic law known to all successful gamblers. Winning and losing come in streaks; in fact all incidents seem to arrange themselves in sequences as if one accident magnetically attracts similar occurences. Keep your eyes open and you will see this law in operation. If you just

* Written as a Foreword to *The Victim's Datebook*.

miss one train you are that much more likely to just miss another; see one man walking down the street talking to himself and you will probably see another; encounter one rude clerk or waiter and you will encounter another who will use exactly the same words. Look through a newspaper: two people on the same day drowned in bathtubs; similar fires and accidents . . . (didn't I already read that story?) or a run of fatalities all the same age. Thursday, May 18, 1979: killed in a plane crash . . . single engine plane piloted by Kevin Brown, 22 . . . Man found burned to death was Clyde N. Olsen, 22 . . . Casper man, 22, dies in traffic accident . . . Man, 22, found guilty in beating death . . .

Suppose this is a day a victim died — not just any victim but one with whom you especially identify. Be careful. This is a dangerous day for you. Remember, those who are ignorant of history are condemned to repeat it. The more you know about that victim and his or her death the better. What was the cause of death? What day of the week? What else happened on that day? Last words? I know from a book, *The Death of Jesse James*, that he died on Monday, April 3, 1882 and the temperature was 46 degrees. He was shot while he had taken his guns off to clean a picture.

'That picture's awful dusty,' were his last words.

Well, if you identify with Jesse James, don't let your mother-in-law talk you up a ladder to dust off a picture on April 3. Watch your driving on the day James Dean was wiped out — and leave your scarf at home on Isadora Duncan's last day.

When Malcolm X arrived at the auditorium on the day he was shot his step lacked its usual vigor, as if he were dead already. Brothers, that's a day to stay home. Bobby Kennedy had a mysterious fainting fit on stage two days before he was killed. A week before Dallas some woman got within two feet of JFK and took his picture.

'She might have assassinated the President,' an official stated flatly.

This victim datebook will call your attention to things like that. If I were a politician in danger of assassination and someone got within two feet of me I'd fire every bodyguard in my entourage and borrow some guns from de Gaulle. Nobody ever got within two feet of Le Général. And I'd stay the hell out of Dallas on November 22.

Hemingway should have known better than to be flying in a light plane in the vicinity of Kilimanjaro. The brain damage he suffered in that crash prompted his suicide a few years later. He put a 12-gauge shotgun against his forehead and tripped both triggers.

'*White white white as far as the eye can see ahead a blinding flash of white the snows of Kilimanjaro!*'

The victim datebook may save you a lot of trouble that way; it may even save your life. Consider the possibility of failure or misfortune and you have already been to the course of both. Suppose you are going to a crucial meeting. *First* consider everything that can go wrong. *Then* consider how the meeting would be successful. Confronting the possibility of failure keys in success. (Performers will tell you that the worse the stage fright the better the performance.)

The victim datebook can also serve as a rich source of conversational gambits.

'Happy birthday, Mr Brown . . . rather amusing coincidence . . . 2 years ago to the day a man named Brown dropped dead in this restaurant right where you're sitting now . . . In the midst of life what?'

Everyone is a victim in the end. Perhaps the publishers of the Datebook should sell future space like cemetery plots. Reserve your date now.

My Experiences with Wilhelm Reich's Orgone Box

I built my first orgone accumulator on a farm near Pharr, Texas in the spring of 1949. I was living in the Rio Grande valley with my friend Kells Elvins, reading Wilhelm Reich, and we decided to build an accumulator out in Kells' orange grove. In a few days we had put up a wooden box about eight feet high and lined it with galvanized iron. Inside was an old icebox which you could get inside and pull on top so that another box of sheet steel descended over you. In this way the effect was presumably heightened by an accumulator inside an accumulator. Kell's wetbacks watched dubiously from a distance, muttering something in Spanish about 'Brujerias' — witchcraft.

Kerouac described my orgone box in *On the Road* — a pretty good trick, as he never set foot on the South Texas farm. He had me taking a shot of morphine and going out to 'moon over his navel'. The fact is that I was not using junk at that time, and even if I had been I certainly would not have done so in an orgone accumulator. Kerouac even went so far as to write that 'Old Bull thought his orgone accumulator would be improved if the wood he used was as organic as possible, so he tied bushy bayou leaves and twigs to his mystical outhouse.' Like so much of Jack's writing, this makes a good story but is actually pure fiction. When he visited me I was living in Algiers, across the river from New Orleans, in a little house laid out like a railroad flat and raised up on the marshy lot by concrete blocks. In Algiers I had practically no front yard at all, and was far too busy with a habit to build an accumulator.

Neal Cassady did visit me at the South Texas farm, but never used the orgone box. Since Kerouac presumably got the story of my first accumulator from Cassady, whose tendency to exaggerate rivalled Jack's, it's a wonder they didn't have me throwing orgies in the accumulator for the amusement of the wetbacks. But the orgone box does have a definite sexual effect; I also made a little one from any army-style gas-can covered with burlap and cotton wool and wrapped around with gunny sack, and it was a potent sexual tool. The orgones would stream out of the nozzle of the gas can. One day I got into the big accumulator and held the little one over my joint and came right off. That used to be one of Cocteau's party tricks — take off all his clothes, lie down, and come off, no hands.

Wilhelm Reich was, so far as I know, the first investigator to apply the scientific method to sexual phenomena and actually measure the electrical charge of an orgasm and correlate these measurements with the subjective experience of pleasure or displeasure. There is the pleasurable orgasm, like a rising sales graph, and there is the unpleasurable orgasm, slumping ominously like the Dow Jones in 1929. For these experiments he was expelled from Norway, the traditional Scandinavian tolerance seemingly unable to assimilate such experiments. Perhaps any basic experiments into the human condition are dangerous to the tissue of false pride and misconception with which the human animal compulsively covers his nakedness.

Reich advocated the use of orgone therapy both as a preventive and as the best treatment for active cancer. He considered that cancer occurs when the electrical charge at the surface of the cells falls to a suffocation point. To offset this condition and tone up the cells, he developed orgone therapy. This therapy was rejected out of hand without trial by the medical establishment. Reich's books were burned, his machines destroyed, and he died in prison.

Reich's therapy is harmless and need not conflict with any other form of therapy. It could in fact be administered during the time it takes to get biopsies and arrange for an operation. It could also be used in hopeless cases and most importantly in precancerous conditions. By removing even the possibility of this form of treatment, the Federal authorities have taken a heavy responsibility on themselves, especially in view of the fact that independent researchers like Mr C.D. Cone are now corroborating some of Reich's findings.

Who is the FDA to deprive cancer patients of any treatment that could be efficacious? I am sure that most cancer patients would be glad to try any form of treatment that did not interfere with orthodox methods. The decision should rest, certainly, with the individual cancer patient and not with the FDA or the DAR. It has occurred to this investigator that orgone energy might be concentrated and directed in an effort to disperse the miasma of idiotic prurience and anxiety that blocks any scientific investigation of sexual phenomena.

When I took, some years ago, a loft in lower SoHo my friend David Prentice was building some furniture for me. We decided to make an orgone accumulator and assemble it in the loft. He built a plywood box big enough to put a chair inside, with a layer of cork and a galvanized steel lining. On the outside he draped half a dozen ratty old rabbit-fur coats, to beef up the orgone charge. The rabbit coats give the box a surrealist look, very organic, like a fur-lined bathtub. I spent fifteen to twenty minutes a day in the box meditating, with the comfortable feeling that I was at least cutting down the odds of contracting cancer. It had occurred to me that the effect could be greatly enhanced by using *magnetized* iron and building the accumulator in a pyramid shape. If pyramids can prevent meat from decaying, they might do as much for you.

How You Stop Smoking

(A Book Review of the million-seller, *How to Stop Smoking*. Herbert Brean, Pocket Books 1975; 1st publ. 1959). In the form of a television ad.

It is interesting that tobacco, the most available and widely used of all drugs, should turn out to have the most conclusive mortality statistics. Such statistics on cannabis would undoubtedly be used to justify and continue existing laws, but no one so far has proposed to outlaw the manufacture, sale, and possession of tobacco.

The statistics on tobacco use and lung cancer, though widely publicized, seem to have little effect on smokers, even those of middle age or older who are quite aware of the immediate risk of lung cancer. They know they ought to stop, but they don't know *how* to stop. This book — (holds book up to camera) — tells you how. The writer offers a money-back guarantee: 'If you don't give up smoking after reading this book and trying its proven methods, you get your money back.'

I bought this book. I followed the instructions. I stopped smoking — after fifteen years, two packs a day. Previous to reading Brean's book I had never got beyond a few muddled attempts to ration myself down to one pack a day and never doing it, and was deeply convinced that it was hopeless to try. What magic words in this book enabled me, and many others who have read this book, to stop smoking?

The first step is to be sure you want to stop. Yes, think of everything you *like* about smoking. If you still want to stop, read on and you will. If you don't want to stop, turn on another program.

Start thinking about it. Think of it coolly and calmly, without fear or hopelessness. Many others have done it — you can too. Consider the whole idea objectively. Don't try to make even a tentative resolution. Think about it — that's all. You can't change it? It's like the weather? Take a long cool look at that tobacco weather, and see whether you like it. Look at yourself looking forward to the next cigarette — you get your little treat after you come back from the supermarket, hustled from one cigarette to another from morning till night, don't own your own hands, always crawling into your pocket and sneaking out another, you don't even remember smoking another and another until you see the pile of butts in the ashtray, first pack almost gone at three in the afternoon . . . mouth raw, he goes into momentary panic when he finds only three Senior Service left . . . thank God — he finds an untouched pack in a drawer. Cancer sighs with relief from young oat cells need the tar and cyanide and nicotine to live and breathe.

Now just seeing all this without any reaction, from a point of zero cigarettes (you are *thinking* about stopping), you have already stopped; by reaching the point where you can look at it, a point in future time when you will stop smoking. You want to stop, and you are convinced that you can't — without even making the attempt, without even *considering* the attempt? You doubt you could even sit in 'Non-Smoking' on a three-hour air trip, and you beat John Wayne to the draw when the no-smoking sign clicks off.

And think about those cancer statistics. Don't scare yourself, just think about them. Already doctors are talking about an epidemic. Idea for a science fiction novel here: The steady increase in cancer becomes a tidal wave. Accelerated cancer reduces the smoker to a tumor in a few weeks. Tobacco turns out to be a long-range weapon of the Venusians to exterminate the natives. The breed could land by killing or weakening cancer antibodies — they are going to hatch out of the tumors. Don't scare yourself, just look: You are looking right at cancer. Plop of diseased lung into a bloody trough . . .

'A (cigarette brand) is *great* after major surgery,' said Doctor Caspar Higgin, after removing a lung from his twin brother.

So you've thought about it. Now make a list of everything you don't like about smoking and carry it around with you. By thinking about it you already have a list. Now pick your time and *stop*. No cutting down, no rationing: *Stop. Do not permit yourself one single exception*.

The first day you don't take it seriously — you might start again tomorrow — but somehow you don't. By the third day you know you have actually stopped, and that you prefer the way you are now to the way you were when you smoked. Now you can see the dreary sordid slavery of tobacco. Why, one respected matron who tried to stop rushed out of her house at midnight in her pajamas, quite mad for cigarettes, cribbing in gutters and ash cans . . . And Oscar Wilde often encountered a young friend on the floor as they both searched the trash for usable butts.

Observing what happens when you stop smoking will tell you a lot about what the actual function of smoking is. For one thing, people light up to cover pain, worry, embarrassment. Remember the advertisements for Murad cigarettes?

'Embarrassing moments . . .' (Her husband returns unexpectedly, etc.)

'Be nonchalant: light a Murad.'

And when the doctor tells you you got oat cell cancer in both lungs, be nonchalant, light a Murad — you might as well.

I see the old smoking Burroughs dim jerky far away in a 1920's comedy where it's always two in the morning and languid aristocrats yawn out smoke rings. It was put down in the ads as glamorous, a badge of manhood and sophistication. I see it now as a dirty, ruinous, slobbish habit. Smokers of the world, look in the mirror. 'These are unsightly tricks' — Doctor Strangelove slaps his creeping hand away from his pocket.

No-smoking Rallies could be organized . . .

'Oh I just know I had to stop . . .'

'It came to me real sudden, "I don't have to do that" . . .'

'I know, I know, I know . . .'

They wallow in congratulatory heaps until attacked by the displaced tobacco workers. But they can run so much faster . . . they scatter laughing gaily. Tobacco posters rot and peel and flap in the wind. Radiant pop stars strip off tobacco plants. The tobacco industry is ruined. Oh, there were a few people who smoked five cigarettes a day — they can grow their own for all the money to be made off them and some cranky old pipe-smokers. It catches on like mad: a whole film is made in which nobody smokes. Soon it is as bad form to flash a cigarette package as a mink stole.

'In their insensate fury they could turn on other products,' a former president of Tobacco Amalgamated warned bluntly. Yes indeed — on a lot of old products. When you stop smoking, all habits are called into question. You begin to take a long cool look at everything you think and do. How much of your thinking and doing is predicated on a conviction that you can't change? You have just proven to yourself that you can. So why stop with cigarettes? You can give up anything or anybody.

'Sorry . . . you're an old bad habit.'

169

Those of you who have listened to this program want to stop smoking, otherwise you wouldn't have listened. Buy Brean's book *How To Stop Smoking*. Follow the Instructions in that book. And you will stop smoking.

The Maugham Curse

Notes on Ted Morgan's book, *Maugham*, which is a great deal more interesting than Maugham himself. Robin Maugham thought that his uncle Willy had made a Devil's bargain. The Devil's Bargain is always a fool's bargain and especially for the artist. Because the Devil does not, in fact *cannot*, dispense quality merchandise. He can make you the most famous, the most widely read, the richest writer in the world, but he cannot make you the best writer. Or even a good writer.

And Maugham was acutely conscious of his failures as an artist. Maugham expected to be placed in the very first rank of the second-raters. Sorry, Mr Maugham, there is no such category. Even the position of the second-rater is earned by some first-rate work. A second-rater is an uneven or specialized performer. I can think of writers I read years ago and have forgotten the writers name and the title. But I can remember a chapter, a paragraph, maybe just a phrase, that really shines. Without such flashes a voluminous output of well written volumes counts for little. I have postulated that the function of art is to show us the way to space. Applying this touchstone to words, Maugham fails as an artist. He is competent but never magical. It is many years since I read Maugham and he does not reread well. I cannot bring myself to care about his characters because he obviously does not care himself. Contrast the loving care which Conrad dedicates to Lord Jim. And the way in which Genet transfigures his pimps and thieves. Genet said that the writer must assume a terrible responsibility for the characters he creates. It is obvious that Maugham felt no such responsibility. Conrad and Genet are writers for the space age. Maugham is not.

Robin Maugham says that Willie was haunted by something evil. He relates this incident which took place in Maugham's last years. He (Willie) was staring towards the door. His face was contorted with fear and he was trembling violently. 'Who's that coming into the room?' he asked. Willie's face was ashen as he began to shriek 'Go away! I'm not ready! I'm not dead yet I tell you!'

171

'I looked around but the room was empty,' said Robin.

Perhaps if Maugham could have written about that . . . But it wasn't in the bargain. Shortly before his death, he asked Robin, 'You don't believe one can lose one's soul so completely in this life that there is nothing left do you?' Robin dutifully assured him that this was not possible, like reassuring a cancer victim that he will recover.

Conrad remarks in one of his illuminating introductory notes that the Devil's Bargain is always a fool's bargain. And especially a fool's bargain for a writer since a writer deals in *qualitative data*. A man whose goals are solid and realizable — wealth, power, fame, position — may feel that he has gotten his soul's worth at least until the fine print is spelled out on him. But an artist stands to gain nothing from such a bargain.

Maugham, one feels, sold out at birth. There is nothing that he might have done if he hadn't made the Bargain. What I remember about Maugham, and I read them all as they came out, sometimes in the Taushnitz edition in my *pension*, are a few sentences . . .

'If someone calls and leaves a message that it's important you can be sure it is important to them and not to you.'

'The way to eat well in England is to eat breakfast three times a day.'

Is this *all*? Well, almost all. To my mind what a novelist does is create characters. Look at Maugham's characters . . . The hero of *The Razor's Edge*, I can't remember his name to start with . . . a nothing, appropriately played by the nothing Tyrone Power in the film.

Blake in *The Narrow Corner*. They don't live. They don't engage our affection. We don't *like* them. We feel nothing for them. The reason is very simple: no feeling, no love went into them. Compare these pale lifeless characters with Lord Jim and the Great Gatsby. Consider the care and love that went into these characters. They *shine* with the writer's gift of life. Maugham had no such gift to give. He lost it in the bargain. Only his malicious vignettes come alive at all . . . Roy in *Cakes and Ale* for instance. The closest Maugham ever came to creating a character was with Sadie Thompson, who draws her strength from the actresses who portrayed her. Interesting that Maugham turned down Tallulah Bankhead for the part! Maybe it wasn't in the Contract. She could have been too good.

Obviously Maugham regretted his bargain and sought to deny its implications. It would seem that he didn't even read the large print. For he must have known that the Devil can't make you a good writer. But he can make you a famous writer, a successful writer, a rich writer. And Maugham got his full soul's worth there: the Villa Mauresque. Lunch with the queen. Had he jogged the Devil's arm he could have gotten a Knighthood.

But every writer wants to be a good writer. He may want to be the *best writer*, not in a competitive sense, since writers cannot be compared except in general terms. I mean any writer who is a writer wants to do the best job of writing he can do. And Maugham was a writer. He never made his living in any other way. He *chose* to be a writer, not a doctor or a lawyer or a politician.

So he knew what he had done and consoled himself with his paltry prizes... the perfect martini at one... lunch... guests... nap... walk... cocktails at seven... dinner with guests, oh very distinguished guests like Noel Coward, Winston Churchill and the Duke of Windsor. The Villa Mauresque was the biggest closet on the Riviera in more ways than one.

And one by one back in the closet lays...

Jean Genet said of Julien Green... 'I'l n'a pas le courage d'être ecrivain.' He does not have the courage to be a writer. Parenthetically I do not agree with Genet. I think that *Le Pelerin sur la terre* and *L'autre sommeil* represent first class work in a very difficult genre, the borderline supernatural.

What is the courage Genet refers to?: The courage to face the horrific perils of one of the most dangerous of all professions, involving penalties and exposing oneself to punishments worse than death, much worse.

Old Lady: 'It must be very dangerous to be a writer.'

Writer: 'It is madam and few survive it.'

You can bog down in your style like Mammerstein. You can spend 20 years writing the great book that nobody can read like Joyce. You can standardize a product until it slowly dies for the lack of any good reason to live: the bad Catholic on a mission he doesn't really believe in, debating the desirability or even the feasability of ordering another beer he isn't sure he really wants before the boat docks.

Mr Greene, I was once caught short in a flight diverted from New York to Philadelphia because of weather conditions. There we are grounded, we can't leave the plane because we haven't cleared customs... Three hours... no drinks... no smoking . . . But I have, so I think, an ace in the hole put aside for just such an emergency . . . I reach for *Travels With My Aunt* to ease the horror of my position only to find I have been served a worthless placebo . . . My God, it's terrible thin and empty . . . Sipping champagne on his patio as flowers rain down and 'Lotus Land' I thought . . . He is going to marry a young Indian girl, buy a Dakota and start smuggling whiskey and cigarettes. Is this your heaven Mr Greene? Perhaps the best thing is write a few wowzers and quit like Genet . . . What you do then? Nobody except perhaps a washed-up intelligence agent is less able to survive without his purpose than a dedicated writer. The thought appalls me. Oh, I have other hobbies to ride: guns and weaponry . . . but for that you need money, and I don't have any money except what I make from writing. And that source can dry up at any time . . . Remember an old 1920 song from the early days of motoring:

You're going fine/ Then you see a sign/ With the word sublime/ DETOUR . . .

WRITER'S BLOCK. It hits you heavy and cold as a cop's blackjack on a winter night. Suddenly you can't do anything. You shrink from the typewriter. You turn sick with the sight of your words on paper . . .

> You sit around wondering what it's all about
> You don't make some money going to put you out . . .

WRITER'S BLOCK. We don't like to talk about it . . . 'It just doesn't come any more!' Hemingway said and shot himself. You can't even write a letter. You'd rather do anything else than write. Some people sharpen pencils . . . In the country you can cut wood . . . Anything to put off the dreaded moment: sit down and write . . .

Well maybe it's time to retire. How does a writer retire? Retire to what? Maugham: 'I'm 86 and that's an old party.' A very old party . . . It is pleasant to sit in the sun is it not?' Chilling is it not? Like the old men in St Petersburg looking forward to the next meal and the next shit and sitting on their favorite bench in the sun . . .

And what causes WB? Usually it's overwriting. Your bad writing catching up to you . . . I remember Mary MacCarthy saying about me . . . 'He writes too much . . . ' But I wouldn't listen . . . Went on writing and writing and a lot of it is terrible . . . Then it hits . . . You just have to wait it out . . .

Yessa very dangerous profession . . . They bog down in religion. They become Communists, which is worse because of the basically spurious position of Communism/Progress towards what? Better living standards for a population of decorticated zombies . . . Why? Who cares?

One cannot be dubious of a writer who does too many other things . . . the Renaissance Man syndrome. I felt that if I lived for 300 years I might begin to learn something about writing. What a writer is *actually doing*.

Remembering Jack Kerouac

Jack Kerouac was a writer. That is, he wrote. Many people who call themselves writers and have their names on books are not writers and they can't write, like a bullfighter who makes passes with no bull there. The writer has been there or he can't write about it. And going there, he risks being gored. By that I mean what the Germans aptly call the Time Ghost. For example, such a fragile ghost world as Fitzgerald's Jazz Age — all the sad young men, firefly evenings, winter dreams, fragile, fragile like his picture taken in his 23rd year — Fitzgerald, poet of the Jazz Age. He went there and wrote it and brought it back for a generation to read, but he never found his own way back. A whole migrant generation arose from Kerouac's *On the Road* to Mexico, Tangier, Afghanistan, India.

What are writers, and I will confine the use of this term to writers of novels, trying to do? They are trying to create a universe in which they have lived or where they would like to live. To write it, they must go there and submit to conditions that they may not have bargained for. Sometimes, as in the case of Fitzgerald and Kerouac, the effect produced by a writer is immediate, as if a generation were waiting to be written. In other cases, there may be a time lag. Science fiction, for example, has a way of coming true. In any case, by writing a universe, the writer makes such a universe possible.

To what extent writers can and do act out their writing in so-called real life, and how useful it is for their craft, are open questions. That is, are you making your universe more like the real universe, or are you pulling the real one into yours? Winner take nothing. For example, Hemingway's determination to act out the least interesting aspects of his own writing and to actually be his character, was, I feel, unfortunate for his writing. Quite simply, if a writer insists on being able to do and do well what his characters do, he limits the range of his characters.

However, writers profit from doing something even when done badly. I was, for one short week — brings on my ulcers to think about it — a very bad assistant pickpocket. I decided that a week was enough, and I didn't have the touch, really.

Walking around the wilderness of outer Brooklyn with the Sailor after a mooch (as he called a drunk) came up on us at the end of Flatbush: 'The cops'll beat the shit out of us . . . you have to expect that.' I shuddered and didn't want to expect that and decided right there that I was going to turn in my copy of the Times, the one I would use to cover him when he put the hand out. We always used the same copy — he said people would try to read it and get confused when it was a month old, and this would keep them from seeing us. He was quite a philosopher, the Sailor was . . . but a week was enough before I got what I 'had to expect . . .'

'Here comes one . . . yellow lights, too.' We huddle in a vacant lot . . . Speaking for myself at least, who can always see what I look like from outside, I look like a frightened commuter clutching his briefcase as Hell's Angels roar past.

Now if this might seem a cowardly way, cowering in a vacant lot when I should have given myself the experience of getting worked over by the skinny short cop with the acne-scarred face who looks out of that prowl car, his eyes brown and burning in his head — well, the Sailor wouldn't have liked that, and neither would a White Hunter have liked a client there to get himself mauled by a lion.

Fitzgerald said once to Hemingway, 'Rich people are different from you and me.'

'Yes . . . they have more money.' And writers are different from you and me. They write. You don't bring back a story if you get yourself killed. So a writer need not be ashamed to hide in a vacant lot or a corner of the room for a few minutes. He is there as a writer and not as a character. There is nothing more elusive than a writer's main character, the character that is assumed by the reader to be the writer himself, no less, actually doing the things he writes about. But this main character is simply a point of view interposed by the writer. The main character then becomes in fact another character in the book, but usually the most difficult to see, because he is mistaken for the writer himself. He is the writer's observer, often very uneasy in this role and at a loss to account for his presence. He is an object of suspicion to the world of nonwriters, unless he manages to write them into his road.

Kerouac says in *Vanity of Duluoz*: 'I am not "I am" but just a spy in someone's body pretending these sandlot games, kids in the cow field near St. Rota's Church . . .' Jack Kerouac knew

177

about writing when I first met him in 1944. He was 21; already he had written a million words and was completely dedicated to his chosen trade. It was Kerouac who kept telling me I should write and call the book I wrote *Naked Lunch*. I had never written anything after high school and did not think of myself as a writer, and I told him so. 'I got no talent for writing . . .' I had tried a few times, a page maybe. Reading it over always gave me a feeling of fatigue and disgust, an aversion towards this form of activity, such as a laboratory rat must experience when he chooses the wrong path and gets a sharp reprimand from a needle in his displeasure centers. Jack insisted quietly that I did have talent for writing and that I would write a book called *Naked Lunch*. To which I replied, 'I don't want to hear anything literary.'

Trying to remember just where and when this was said is like trying to remember a jumble of old films. The 1940's seem centuries away. I see a bar on 116th Street here, and a scene five years later in another century: a sailor at the bar who reeled over on the cue of 'Naked Lunch' and accused us — I think Allen Ginsberg was there, and John Kingsland — of making a sneering reference to the Swiss Navy. Kerouac was good in these situations, since he was basically unhostile. Or was it in New Orleans or Algiers, to be more precise, where I lived in a frame house by the river, or was it later in Mexico by the lake in Chapultepec Park . . . there's an island there where thousands of vultures roost apathetically. I was shocked at this sight, since I had always admired their aerial teamwork, some skimming a few feet off the ground, others wheeling way up, little black specks in the sky — and when they spot food they pour down in a black funnel . . .

We are sitting on the edge of the lake with tacos and bottles of beer . . . 'Naked Lunch is the only title,' Jack said. I pointed to the vultures.

'They've given up, like old men in St. Petersburg, Florida . . . Go out and hustle some carrion you lazy buzzards!' Whipping out my pearlhandled .45, I killed six of them in showers of black feathers. The other vultures took to the sky . . . I would act these out with Jack, and quite a few of the scenes that later appeared in Naked Lunch arose from these acts. When Jack came to Tangier in 1957, I had decided to use the title, and much of the book was already written.

In fact, during all those years I knew Kerouac, I can't remember ever seeing him really angry or hostile. It was the sort of smile he gave in reply to my demurrers, in a way you get from a priest who knows you will come to Jesus sooner or later — you can't walk out on the Shakespeare Squadron, Bill.

Now as a very young child I had wanted to be a writer. At the age of 9 I wrote something called *Autobiography of a Wolf*. This early literary essay was influenced by — so strongly as to smell of plagiarism — a little book I had just read called *The Biography of a Grizzly Bear*. There were various vicissitudes, including the loss of his beloved mate . . . in the end this poor old bear slouches into a valley he knows is full of poison gases, about to die . . . I can see the picture now, it's all in sepia, the valley full of nitrous yellow fumes and the bear walking in like a resigned criminal to the gas chamber. Now I had to give my wolf a different twist, so, saddened by the loss of his entire family, he encounters a grizzly bear who kills him and eats him. Later there was something called *Carl Cranbury in Egypt* that never got off the ground, really . . . a knife glinted in the dark valley. With lightning speed Carl V. Cranbury reached for the blue steel automatic . . .

These were written out painfully in longhand with great attention to the script. The actual process of writing became so painful that I couldn't do anything more for Carl Cranbury, as the Dark Ages descended — the years in which I wanted to be anything else but a writer. A private detective, a bartender, a criminal . . . I failed miserably at all these callings, but a writer is not concerned with success or failure, but simply with observation and recall. At the time I was not gathering material for a book. I simply was not doing anything well enough to make a living at it. In this respect, Kerouac did better that I did. He didn't like it, but he did it — work on railroads and in factories. My record time on a factory job was four weeks. And I had the distinction to be actually fired from a defense plant during the War.

Perhaps Kerouac did better because he saw his work interludes simply as a means to buy time to write. Tell me how many books a writer has written . . . we can assume usually 10 times that amount shelved or thrown away. And I will tell you how he spends his time: Any writer spends a good deal of his time alone, writing. And that is how I remember Kerouac — as a writer talking about writers or sitting in a quiet corner with a notebook, writing in longhand. He was also very fast on the typewriter. You feel that he was writing all the time; that writing was the only thing he thought about. He never wanted to do anything else.

If I seem to be talking more about myself than about Kerouac, it is because I am trying to say something about the particular role that Kerouac played in my life script. As a child, I had given up on writing, perhaps unable to face what every writer must: all the bad writing he will have to do before he does any good writing. An interesting exercise would be to collect all the worst writing of any writer — which simply shows the pressures that writers are under to write badly, that is, not write. This pressure is, in part, simply the writer's own conditioning from childhood to think (in my case) white Protestant American or (in Kerouac's case) to think French-Canadian Catholic.

Writers are, in a way, very powerful indeed. They write the script for the reality film. Kerouac opened a million coffee bars and sold a million pairs of Levis to both sexes. Woodstock rises from his pages. Now if writers could get together into a real tight union, we'd have the world right by the words. We could write our own universes, and they would all be as real as a coffee bar or a pair of Levis or a prom in the Jazz Age. Writers could take over the reality studio. So they must not be allowed to find out that they can make it happen. Kerouac understood this long before I did. Life is a dream, he said.

My own birth records, my family's birth records and recorded origins, my athletic records in the newspaper clippings I have, my own notebooks and published books are not real at all; my own dreams are not dreams at all but products of my waking imagination . . . This, then, is the writer's world — the dream made for a moment actual on paper, you can almost touch it, like the endings of *The Great Gatsby* and *On the Road*. Both express a dream that was taken up by a generation.

Life is a dream in which the same person may appear at various times in different roles. Years before I met Kerouac, a friend from high school and college, Kells Elvins, told me repeatedly that I should write and that I was not suited to do anything else. When I was doing graduate work at Harvard in 1938, we wrote a story in collaboration, entitled *Twilight's Last Gleamings*, which I used many years later almost verbatim in *Nova Express*. We acted out the parts, sitting on a side porch of the white frame house we rented together, and this was the birthplace of Doctor Benway.

'Are you all all right?' he shouted, seating himself in the first

180

lifeboat among the women. 'I'm the doctor!'

Years later in Tangier, Kells told me the truth: 'I know I am dead and you are too . . .' Writers are all dead, and all writing is posthumous. We are really from beyond the tomb and no commissions . . . (All this I am writing just as I think of it, according to Kerouac's own manner of writing. He says the first version is always the best.)

In 1945 or thereabouts, Kerouac and I collaborated on a novel that was never published. Some of the material covered in this lost opus was later used by Jack in *The Town and the City* and *Vanity of Duluoz*. At that time, the anonymous gray character of William Lee was taking shape: Lee, who is there just so long and long enough to see and hear what he needs to see and hear for some scene or character he will use 20 or 30 years later in his writing. No, he wasn't there as a private detective, a bartender, a cotton farmer, a pickpocket, an exterminator; he was there in his capacity as a writer. I did not know that until later. Kerouac, it seems, was born knowing. And he told me what I already knew, which is the only thing you can tell anybody.

I am speaking of the role Kerouac played in my script, and the role I played in his can be inferred from the enigmatically pompous Hubbard Bull Lee portrayals, which readily adapt themselves to the scenes between Carl and Doctor Benway in *Naked Lunch*. Kerouac may have felt that I did not include him in my cast of characters, but he is of course the anonymous William Lee as defined in our collaboration — a spy in someone else's body where nobody knows who is spying on whom. Sitting on a side porch, Lee was there in his capacity as a writer. So Doctor Benway told me what I knew already: 'I'm the doctor . . .'

Beckett and Proust

I recall a personal visit to Beckett. John Calder, my publisher and Beckett's, was the intermediary for a short, not more than half an hour audience. This was in Berlin. Beckett was there directing one of his new plays. Allen Ginsberg, Susan Sontag and myself were there for a reading. Also present in the visiting party were Fred Jordan and Professor Hoellerer, a professor of English literature at Berlin University.

Beckett was polite and articulate. It was, however, apparent to me at least that he had not the slightest interest in any of us, nor the slightest desire to ever see any of us again. We had been warned to take our own liquor as he would proffer none. So we had brought along a bottle of whisky. Beckett accepted a small drink which he sipped throughout the visit. Asking the various participants first what Beckett said, and what the whole conversation was about seems to elicit quite different responses. Nobody seems to remember at all clearly. It was as if we had entered a hiatus of disinterest. I recall that we did talk about my son's recent liver transplant and the rejection syndrome. I reminded Beckett of our last meeting in Maurice Girodias' restaurant. On this occasion we had argued about the cut-ups, and I had no wish to renew the argument. So it was just 'yes', 'Maurice's restaurant'. Allen, I believe, asked Beckett if he had ever given a reading of his work. Beckett said 'No'.

There was some small talk about the apartment placed at his disposal by the Academy: a sparsely furnished duplex overlooking the Tiergarten. I said the zoo was very good, one of the best, with nocturnal creatures in diaramas, like their natural habitat. They even have flying foxes. Beckett nodded, as if willing to take my word for this. I think there was some discussion of Susan Sontag's cancer. I looked at my watch. Some one asked Allen or Fred for the time. We got up to go. Beckett shook hands politely.

The whole inward/outward, introverted/extroverted dichotomy is an either/or imposition on data which isn't either/or and cannot be accurately confined in either/or terms. The whole inward/outward, introverted/extroverted dichotomy is misleading and inaccurate. The data of perception simply cannot be accurately confined in either/or terms. All experience is both objective and subjective. Obviously, there has to be a subject to experience, and something for the subject to experience. There are of course shades and degrees of emphasis.

Some people are undoubtedly more concerned with interpsychic data than others. We can see it as a spectrum with various degrees of attention. And it seems to me that Proust and Beckett are at opposite ends of the spectrum. Proust is principally concerned with time. Beckett is virtually timeless. Proust is concerned with minute descriptions of objects and characters with their sets. What do the characters, if they could be so called in Beckett, even look like, beside being awkward and not young? And the sets? What sets? His writing can be taking place anywhere. The Unnameable in its bottle could be in Paris, Hong Kong or Helsinki. Proust's characters are firmly rooted in place and time. They are French high society: Dukes and Barons who all have long essential names. They are their names. But Watt, Malone, Murphy? The Unnameable?

I am very much closer to Proust than to Beckett. I am very much concerned with the creation of character. In fact I can say that this is my principal preoccupation. If I am remembered for anything, it will be for my characters, for Doctor Benway and A.J., for Audrey and Kim Carsons, for the Vigilante and the Heavy Metal Kid, for Hamburger Mary and Salt Chunk Mary, for the Fag, and the Beagle and the Sailor and Pantapon Rose, for Old Ike and Tio Mary and Loa la Chata, for Daddy Long Legs and the Rube.

There is no time in Beckett. Take *Waiting for Godot*. The characters can wait forever. Godot never comes. Take *Watt* or *Malone Dies*. There's no time. Take *The Unnameable. The Unnameable* is timeless. Only that which can be named or designated is subject to time. Proust is all names and all time. There is no Memory in Beckett. Even *Krapp's Last Tape* has no memory in the usual sense of associated recall, but rather, a mechanical process set in motion by a jar or vibration: the closing of or opening of a door.

Beckett is quite literally inhuman. You will look in vain for human motivations of jealousy, hate or love. Even fear is absent. Nothing remains of human emotions except weariness and distress, tinged with remote sadness.

183

Proust, on the other hand, reflects all manner of emotion, fear, contempt, hatred, love. In fact, the whole of *A la recherche du temps perdu* is an elaborate and beautiful structure, lovingly created and exposing, as he himself said, the poetry in snobbery.

That he was a snob humanizes Proust in a way that Beckett is never humanized. Beckett's basic motivations are extremely obscure. Proust, in a sense, wrote to encompass and make appropriate the society that never completely accepted him. Or that is certainly an aspect. But Beckett?

Perhaps writing is simply natural to him, and an expression of his being that he is somehow obligated to make. The nature of this obligation is difficult to discern. Perhaps he means something quite different from what is ordinarily conveyed by the word obligation. Are we obligated to breathe? He comes, I think, as near as a man can to breathing his work. Personal impressions . . . Completely aloof, but not at all prickly or ill at ease. We talked about a number of questions. And it seems that everyone present had quite a different account of the meeting. What did he actually say?

Beckett violates all the rules and conventions of the novelist: arbitrary rules, to be sure, which evolved in the late 18th century and solidified in the 19th century.

There is no suspense in Beckett. Beckett is above suspense. There are no cliff-hangers at the end of each chapter. There are no characters as such, and certainly no character development. He is perhaps the purest writer who has ever written. There is nothing there but the writing itself.

There are no tricks, no adornment, nothing with which the reader can identify. It is all moving inward rather than outward, inward to some final inwardness, some ultimate core. Just as the physicists progress from inwards, so Beckett's range is always smaller and more precise. *Endgame* divides the psyche into persons to act out the endgame of division and the futile attempt to end the game which cannot be ended without ending all the characters as well, since they are all part of the same organism.

Proust is at the other end of the spectrum. Characters and character development, along with the creation of elaborate sets and realistic dialogue.

Beckett has, in effect, no dialogue, no ear for dialogue. He doesn't need it. And there is no time for Beckett, or not time as we know it. Take *Endgame*. No time is possible since there is only one character and time is change relative to other persons and objects. Whereas in Proust, time is everything. The memory traces evocations of memory on lines of association. It's all Pavlov.

Now Proust contructed this elaborate mechanical toy of high society puppets, bowing in and out of rooms and corridors and terraces and gardens — a phantom charade, whereas Beckett does not admit of any separate being outside of his own area of perception.

If the role of a novelist is to create characters and the sets in which his characters live and breathe, then Beckett is not a novelist at all. There is no suspense in Beckett: it is all taking place in some grey limbo, and there is also no set. Is it happening in Paris, Berlin, South America? It doesn't matter. There are no characters and no sets. It seems rather to be the endgame of the writer coming at least to grips with his role as ventriloquist reading his lines to dummies.

In Beckett we can see them at last, with all the tawdry alterations and the false moustache. But it is always Monsieur Proust who gets his final revenge on the society that never quite accepted him. He accepted it completely, and it was then his. It has no other existence. They all wind up as Mr Proust's dummies.

Beckett refuses to play. The Dummy is now seen as the dummy. *Malone Dies*. Who killed him? Who created him? *The Unnameable*? Who didn't name it? *Waiting for Godot*. Who wrote Godot? Now the ventriloquist's nightmare is when his dummy starts talking on his own. Suppose a writer's character should start writing on his own? Not the same thing. Spare me a lot of trouble. Have to reserve the right of veto, you know old thing, could have some tripe creep in out over or under my name. Good chap, fine old thing, knew you'd see it my way, hang it all, have to meet in the middle, agree to disagree and all that. So back to Proust.

Like Proust I am very much concerned with Time and Memory; with tracing the lines of association and the intersection of points of memory. I am very concerned with sets, and objects; with scenic landscapes, and rooms, and streets. Where is the landscape in Beckett? Where are the rivers, the swamp, the cities, the rooms, the streets? And dialogue in Beckett — does it exist? It certainly exists in my work. I have an ear for dialogue. And so many phrases are phrases I heard from someone. 'All a Jew wants to do is doodle

185

a Christian girl.' 'Going to give you the chance, extraordinary.' 'He was an individual.' 'Rabies in the worst form there is.'

Beckett closes off whole areas of experience. These areas simply don't interest him. Like the visit. He was meticulously polite and not at all nervous of or of making the visitors nervous. But clearly he was not at all interested in the visitors. Clearly he had not the slightest desire to see any of them ever again. You could imagine his turning in disinterest from an extra-terrestrial.

I am concerned with characters and names and sets. Interzone, New York City, South America, Mexico.

Graham Greene

In 1956 I was stranded in Algiers. I was trying to get back to Tangier, but it was during the civil war and there were no planes, so I had to spend two weeks there. I used to eat lunch in the milk bar. It was a small place with mirrors on the walls, square pillars covered with mirrors, and great jars full of fruit juice, salads, ice cream, bananas and so forth. A month after I left, there was an explosion in the milk bar, and Brion Gysin arrived just a few minutes after the bomb. He described the incredible scene for me: people with arms and legs blown off, covered with blood, brains, maraschino cherries, passion-fruit, bananas and whipped cream, and mirror shards. And Graham Greene gives an identical description of a milk bar explosion in Vietnam.

The Heart of the Matter is the Graham Greene book most closely related to my story *The Health Officer*. This takes place in Central Africa, and concerns Major Scobie, a police official and a bad Catholic, of course. This Scobie is one of these types that dislikes other people and therefore feels guilty towards them because he doesn't care about them. So he is always bending over backwards not to hurt people, and winds up doing much more damage than any wilfull and selfish person can do. No one does more harm than people who feel bad about doing it, in personal relations or anywhere else.

Scobie has a faithful servant named Ali, who has nursed him through bouts of fever and saved his life a few times. There is also in this town a Syrian operator, who has a shop and a warehouse and is into smuggling and receiving stolen goods and anything to make a dollar. He is constantly trying to get to Major Scobie. So Scobie drops in to buy a bottle of whisky: 'Ah, but there is no charge, Major Scobie . . . please take a case, and some perfume for your wife.'

'No thanks. I'll pay for one bottle. And one of these days you're going to find my foot up your fat ass.'

'I should be sorry to think so, Major Scobie. I have for you a warm heart. If you ever need money . . .'

187

It's a good description of the operator: 'He had a face that was both sincere and untrustworthy.' This goes on for years, the Major fighting off whisky and dresses and perfume and offers of an interest-free loan, but the time comes when he does need money to keep his former girlfriend from coming from Africa and to avoid a scene with his wife. He doesn't want either of them to be hurt, you understand, since this sort of thing upsets him, and he doesn't like to be upset. So he borrows the money from the operator.

'Interest? Of course not, Major. Pay me when you can.'

Well, no sooner does the Major have the money in his pocket than he starts paying. 'Oh Major, a small matter . . . a consignment held up at Customs over the weekend. A note from you . . .' After that, the Major gets in deeper and deeper, more and more consignments to be passed through without inspection, and other matters too, letters to be sent by the Major so they won't be opened by the censor. Finally the Major is worried about Ali, who may have sussed out some of this. He goes to see the operator. This is the highlight of the book, this passage:

'Ah Major, I assure you there is no danger. A gentleman like you should not worry about such trifles. Excuse me a moment.' Of course the operator is sending his boys to take care of Ali; Scobie really knows what's happening, but he can't admit it to himself. I mean, he's getting someone else to do his dirty work for him, and he can't even admit it to himself — how low can you get? Then the operator comes back and says, 'And now Major we will talk of serious things . . . God, the family, and Shakespeare.' A scream offstage —

'What was that?'

'Do not concern yourself, Major. People fighting in the streets. They are animals, these people . . .'

Cutting Up Characters

Re-reading Joseph Conrad's *Under Western Eyes*, I find it stands up much better than I remembered. And I see the precise parallels between Razumov's interview with Councillor Mikulin in *Under Western Eyes* and Carl's interview with Doctor Benway in *Naked Lunch*, the chapter entitled 'The Examination'.

Razumov has braced himself to confront the tough cop, General T—. Instead he is taken before the con cop, Councillor Mikulin. Razumov has placed himself in the category of informer by turning in Haldin. As he will find, this is not an easy pigeon-hole to escape from, and in fact Councillor Mikulin has no intention of allowing him to escape.

The con dick does a little dance step . . . 'Why don't you make the man a proposition? That's the way General — you play fair with him and he'll play fair with you.'

Councillor Mikulin and Doctor Benway both use the little dance step of the unfinished sentence; Mikulin: 'I comprehend in a measure your . . . But indeed you are mistaken in what you . . . Though as a matter of fact . . . Religious belief of course is a great . . . And so you say he believed in . . . That's of course . . . Naturally some curiosity was bound to arise . . . Everybody I am sure can . . .'

Doctor Benway: 'The Kleiberg-Stanislouski test . . . a diagnostic tool . . . in certain cases useful . . . I do hope not necessary . . . indicative at least in a negative sense . . . certain contagious diseases . . . relatively rare . . . such marriages often result in . . . there must have been . . . and so . . .'

Here is Razumov's meeting with Mikulin: 'The mild gaze rested on him, not curious, not inquisitive — certainly not suspicious — almost without expression. In its passionless persistence there was something resembling sympathy.'

And Benway: 'For the first time the doctor's eyes flickered across Carl's face, eyes without any emotion Carl had ever experienced in himself or seen in another — at once cold and intense, predatory and impersonal . . .' The same bureaucrat brought from 1906 to 1984, just a little further out in the open. As Razumov will find, Councillor Mikulin is also predatory in his dim passionless way.

Razumov's vision of his brain suffering on the rack . . . 'It is not to be seriously supposed that Razumov had actually dozed off and had dreamed in the presence of Councillor Mikulin, of an old print of the Inquisition.'

And from Carl's examination in *Naked Lunch*: 'Carl dozed off. He was opening a green door. Benway: "Do you often doze off like that? In the middle of a sentence?" Carl: "I wasn't asleep, that is . . ." Benway: "You weren't?"'

Razumov: 'The whole affair is becoming too comical altogether for my taste. A comedy of errors, phantoms, and suspicions. It's positively indecent . . .' 'Councillor Mikulin turned an attentive ear. "Did you say phantoms?" he murmured.'

Carl: 'It's just that the whole thing is unreal. I'm going now, you can't force me to stay.'

Razumov: 'But, really, I must claim the right to be done once and for all with that man. And in order to accomplish this I shall take the liberty . . .' Razumov on his side of the table bowed slightly to the seated bureaucrat. '. . . to retire — simply retire.'

Carl's examination: 'He was walking across the room towards the door. A creeping numbness dragged his legs. The door seemed to recede . . .'

Under Western Eyes: Razumov walked to the door, thinking 'Now he must show his hand. He must ring and have me arrested before I am out of the building, or he must let me go. And either way . . .'

Benway: 'Where can you go, Carl?'

Mikulin: 'An unhurried voice said — "Kirylo Sidorovitch."'

Carl: 'Out — away, through the door.'

Mikulin: 'Razumov at the door turned his head. "To retire," he repeated. "Where to?" asked Councillor Mikulin softly.'

Benway: 'The Green Door, Carl?'

As you see, the end is almost verbatim, and I was thinking of this chapter in *Under Western Eyes* when I wrote the chapter on Carl and Doctor Benway. There's no reason not to use a framework or even words from another writer if they fit in a different setting, and this is done repeatedly. Both chapters are suitable for film treatment, and cutting back and forth between them would I think be a very effective device.

Councillor Mikulin — 1900's sets, pen holders, signet rings, gold-plated telephone ... Doctor Benway — cold clinical Swedish modern set ... The two faces flickering in and out, Benway's face projected onto Mikulin's with Mikulin's voice, Mikulin's voice in Benway's face. Mikulin's face with Benway's voice ... Antony Balch and I performed this experiment of projecting his face onto mine and my face onto his, then mixing faces and voices in various combinations, in a film called *Bill and Tony*.

A Review of the Reviewers

Critics constantly complain that writers are lacking in standards, yet they themselves seem to have no standards other than personal prejudice for literary criticism. To use an analogy: suppose the Michelin Inspectors were equally devoid of consensual criteria for judging food. Here is one inspector . . . 'food superlative, service impeccable, kitchen spotless' and another about the same restaurant . . . 'food abominable, service atrocious, kitchen filthy'. Another inspector strips an Italian restaurant of its stars because he doesn't like Italian cooking. Another would close a restaurant because he disapproves of the chef's private life or the political opinions of the proprietor or complains that the chicken on his plate is not roast beef.

Admittedly it is more difficult to set up standards for literary criticisms but such standards do exist. Mathew Arnold set up three criteria for criticism: 1. What is the writer trying to do? 2. How well does he succeed in doing it? Certainly no one can be justly condemned for not doing what he does not intend to do. 3. Does the work exhibit 'high seriousness'? That is, does it touch on basic issues of good and evil, life and death and the human condition. I would also apply a fourth criteria I learned at the age of twelve. I had written a romantic story about a thirsty traveller who sees a mirage of water and dies from disappointment when it fades. It so happened that a professional writer was staying with the family next door. I cannot remember his name but he had published a novel and was therefore a hero to me. I submitted this childish effort to him and he left a note which was delivered after he had departed for New York and the glamorous life I thought that all writers must lead: '*Write about what you know*. More writers fail because they try to write about things they don't know than for any other one reason. I do not know whether you have ever seen a mirage. I feel reasonably certain that you have never seen a man die from seeing one.'

Now apply these criteria to *The Godfather*: 1. What is the

writer trying to do? He is trying to entertain and tell a story and to give the reader some insights into the workings of the mafia. 2. Does he succeed in doing this? He succeeds admirably. 3. Does the book possess 'high seriousness'? Yes. Some very profound things are said about power. He also points up the contrast between personal responsibility and the lack of responsibility that hides behind such phrases as national security. The Godfather assumes responsibility for the murders he orders. His button men even enjoy these murders. Nobody does more harm than those who feel bad about doing it. Godfathers defend us from a 'difficult decision' in the Pentagon. 4. Does the writer know what he is writing about? Obviously he does and this is what gives the book its impact. The reader immediately senses that the writer has *been there*, that these are actual events and people he is describing.

Now here is a critic who doesn't like Italian cooking . . . 'This book is completely devoid of life enhancing qualities. The writer subjects us to one scene of brutal violence and sexual depravity after the other until one is literally numb and in the end abysmally bored. His preoccupation with Sonny's enormous member is a transparent compensation for his own failing sexual and artistic powers. He emerges as the arch apologist for murder and gangsterism attempting to stifle the nauseating stench of red wine and garlic under the silken robes and perfumes of a Renaissance court. Clearly he would plunge America into Neolithic savagery. Fortunately the vast majority of Americans retain sufficient sanity to reject his message and it is to be hoped his book as well. This is not a book to read. It is a book to be consigned to a cesspool or buried under a stone leaving free access to rats, insects and other crawling things, who if they cannot read can at least eat the filth off these pages.' If this seems exaggerated, the bit about the stone is quoted almost verbatim from a review of *Nova Express* in the Chicago *Tribune* by someone named Sullivan. Is this literary criticism or is it the foul-breathed curses of a toothless crone?

'Toad that under cold stone
Days and nights has thirty one
Sweltered venom sleeping got . . .'

And here is the same critic some years later . . . 'The fame which Mr Puzo achieved with *The Godfather* is sadly tarnished by his latest book. The Godfather is indeed dead and the hands of his descendants are empty of gifts, at least for the reader.'

Looking through some of the reviews of *EXTERMIN-ATOR!* ...

> Here is St Teresa Bloomingdale screaming from her
> bargain basement ... disgusting, depressing, filth,
> complete immorality, utter degradation ...'

Ho hum. This reviewer is very tired of so-called critics who
would substitute for criticism invective and insults strung
together like so many gibbering maniacs in an asylum.

And here is Anatole Broyard ...

> 'Mr Burroughs for all his worldliness seems to succumb
> to the "secret forces at work" syndrome that
> characterizes so much counterculture thinking.' The
> Watergate scandals would seem to indicate that forces
> which for good reason would prefer to remain secret are
> indeed at work.

> 'There is a caricature of the National Convention in
> Chicago 1968 in which Jean Genet is made to say: "It
> is time for writers to support the rebellion of youth not
> only with their words but with their presence as well."'

Genet was not *made* to say that. He did say it in front of Terry
Southern, Dick Seaver and your reporter at a time when he was
supporting the rebellion of youth with his presence.

> 'It is ironical that Burroughs doesn't realize that if
> Genet ever actually said such a thing he would have to
> be "camping".'

Who is Broyard to speak for Genet and say he would *have to
be* 'camping'. I was there. Broyard wasn't. I doubt if he has the
pleasure of Genet's acquaintance. That Genet was not camping
is clearly indicated by the piece he wrote for *Esquire* on the
Convention, by his support of the Black Panthers, not only with
his words but with his presence, and by his later arrest at a
student demonstration in Paris. In failing to recognize Genet as
the real article Broyard betrays his own confusion.

If critics are to exercise the power they so desperately crave
they will have to arrive at some acceptable standards for
criticism and some conception as to what writing is about.
Many people who call themselves writers and have their names
on books are not writers and they do not write; a bullfighter who
fights a bull is different from a bullshitter who makes passes
with no bull there. The writer has been there or he can't write
about it. Fitzgerald wrote the Jazz Age, all the sad young men,
firefly evenings, winter dreams. He wrote it and brought it back
for a generation to read. But he never found his own way back.

A whole migrant generation rose from *On the Road*. In order to write it the writer must go there and submit to conditions he may not have bargained for. He must take risks. Only those critics who are willing and able to follow him on this journey are competent to judge his work.

There are of course many critics who do maintain high standards and I have certainly received my share of constructive criticism. Writing an honest book review is hard work. I know because I have written book reviews. A review of a thousand words takes me at least ten hours and many revisions to complete. I could turn out an unfair negative review in ten minutes. Anybody could. A computer could do it just as effectively and even quicker since it is only necessary to string together derogatory comments with no regard to applicability. Broyard's review of *EXTERMINATOR!* simply reprograms Philip Toynbee's review of *Naked Lunch*. Toynbee begins by saying he has searched himself carefully for pro-establishment bias, puritanism, prejudice against so-called avant-garde writing and finding himself as clean as the applicants for immortality in the *Egyptian Book of the Dead*, pronounces 'this book boring rubbish'. Switch titles, dust in a few quotes, feed in the Toynbee program and out comes Broyard in ten seconds. Perhaps he has found his true metier as a computer programmer and I hope this consoles him for being redundant.

Light Reading

Audrey always reads in space. Most of the crew didn't, 'preferring to wallow in their own dreams like contented alligators,' Audrey thought, with a touch of cool condescension. He preferred to feed his fantasies with carefully selected input and he made an oddly assorted selection. For this trip to Ba'Dan his books were: *An Outcast of the Islands* by Joseph Conrad; *Fury* by Henry Kuttner; *Brave and Cruel* by Denton Welch; some of his own pungent fever notes (he thought of them as potent spices to be used sparingly); *Brak the Barbarian* by John Jakes; *Anabase* by Saint-John Perse; Herodotus — what a liar he is; *The Shootist* by Glendon Swarthout, and oh yes one line from *Blood Hype* by Alan Foster which belongs up with the lush musky exquisite after taste of slime department, and a drug called Fringe culled from *The High Destiny* by Dan Morgan.

You see there is a method in his selection: *An Outcast of the Islands*: white shadows playing out charades of corruption like so many black and white cartoons against the sombre back drop of torpid rivers, swamps, jungle and sky with its prop thunder and clouds and rain that sloshes down on cue. What a film this book could make. Willems is the able ambitious clerk who falls into a trap old as Eve and deadly as Circe. Driven to restless inactivity by the hostility of Almayer, who fears his influence with Captain Lingard, Willems meets a WOMAN for the first time in his life. 30 years old, content with an unattractive wife, he never thought much about sex, too busy getting on and making money.

'It is written that white fools are the slaves of their passions as they have enslaved us with their guns and their money and their machines and their laws,' says Babalatchi the old one-eyed Malay, what a sententious old bore, worse than Almayer himself, whose thought processes are so basically dull, self directed and heavy that he achieves at times a oneness with the objects of his thought not unlike the detachment of the sage as if a river, the weather, his hatred of Willems and his intrigues to rid himself of this danger to his position, float solid in his mind of their own volition, while he looks on as a remote witness.

'The left shore is very unhealthy,' says Almayer. 'Strange that only the breadth of the river . . . ' He dropped off into deep thoughtfulness as if he had forgotten his grievances in a bitter meditation upon the unsanitary conditions of the virgin forests on the left bank . . . Cut in shots of jungle, river, and sky in the style of 19th century impressionist painting ending with paintings of the Left Bank in Paris like *Le Buveur d'absinthe.*

Although Almayer hates the river and the jungle they touch him more directly than they touch Babalatchi who is encased in his ritualized perceptions. Here Almayer takes his place as an advanced master of deep meditation: 'His arms hanging down on each side of the chair, he sat motionless in a meditation so concentrated and so absorbing with all his power of thought deep within himself that all expression disappeared from his face in an aspect of staring vacancy. The lamp standing on the far side of the table threw a section of a lighted circle on the floor where his outstretched legs stuck out from under the table with feet rigid and turned up like the feet of a corpse. His set face with fixed eyes could also be the face of a corpse but for its vacant yet conscious aspect, the hard the stupid the stony aspect of one not dead but only buried under the dust, ashes and corruption of personal thoughts, of base fears, of selfish desires. Ali glanced down at him and said unconcernedly 'Master finish?'

Almayer there in the lamplight from his dinner table, Ali clearing the table, could also be a 19th century painting, Delacroix perhaps, with the chair and the light by Van Gogh.

Captain Lingard, Lord of the Seas, is a Daddy Warbucks cartoon with a kind and heavy hand. He knows his Malays and that the Malays and Arabs are stylized recordings. They were there before the white man came. Like the river and forest they will be there after the white men are gone.

Yes, Babalatchi knows his white men. 'Ai it is written that all white men are fools.'

Blast off. Everyone in his bunk. The space ship looks rather like a submarine — tiers of bunks and lockers all very functional. Audrey's books have iron filings pressed into the covers which give them an ozony smell. The shelf by his bunk is magnetized to keep his books, possessions and equipment from floating around.

In the timeless silence of space every thought, feeling and perception is immediately translated into spatial terms.

197

Pictures, tastes, smells pop out of the words. He has a feeling of participating in the scenes that rise from the pages in front of his eyes, and at the same time a realization of unreality and distance. Rather like being an actor in a play watching the stage through a telescope.

Very sharp and clear and far away: 'The man who suggested Willems a mistrusted, disliked worn-out European, living on the reluctant toleration of that outpost up that sombre stream which our ship was the only white man's ship to visit, . . . Hollow clean-shaven cheeks, a heavy gray moustache, eyes without any expression whatever, he wandered silently among the houses in daylight almost as dumb as an animal. An air of futile mystery hung over him, something not exactly dark but obviously ugly.' Very much like a burnt out terminal fever case, consumed by the deadly ecstasies of fever delirium, a solid empty body from which the soul has departed.

Audrey leafs through his fever notes. All the crew had had fever at one time or another, it was, like malaria in the tropics, one of the dangers of space travel. Sooner or later you came to terms with it, learned to live with it, or it destroyed you.

In *Fury* by Kuttner — a bad title Audrey thinks, no wonder it went out of print — the deadly temptation takes the form of an organism which by direct neural contact establishes a lethal symbiosis that ensures death in a few years. 'Happy Cloak addicts lasted about two years on the average. The thing was a biological adaptation of an organism found in the Venusian seas. It got its prey by touching it. After that neuro-contact had been established the prey was quite content to be ingested. It was a beautiful garment, a living white like the white of a pearl shimmering with rippling lights, stirring with a terrible ecstatic movement as the lethal symbiosis was established.'

Blood Hype concerns a drug so habit forming that withdrawal involves an excruciatingly painful death. 'Moderate doses produce a "fire fit", an intense burning sensation that adds to the overall pleasure.'

Of course one could come to terms and take it all quite lightly, why he might write an inspirational article for *The Reader's Digest, How I Turned My Fever into a Profitable Part Time Business*, raising miniature Happy Cloaks in a basement aquarium. Choicer than Piranha fish my dear her glow in the dark.

He turns to a story called *The Barn* in Denton Welch's *Brave and Cruel*. How charming and innocent. The boy loosens his pants and chins himself on a beam: 'I rested my chin on the beetle eaten oak. Slowly and gently I felt my trousers slipping. They slid caressingly over my hips and fell with a soft plop to my ankles. I still hung there supported by my chin and my tingling arms. Soft draughts of air blew deliciously against my complete nakedness. Now I am a criminal whose feet have been tied together and whose body has been stripped by the hangman living passionately my idea of a criminal on the gibbet while the rain beat on the barn doors and drops fell from the roof.'

Audrey can see the naked red-haired boy lost back there with little scraps of delight and burning scrolls in your birthday suit. 'Let's go Audrey' stripped naked down to his quivering toes intense burning sensation along the backs of his thighs musty unused barn in the August heat his nuts crinkle to autumn leaves long ago ass going where?

From *Brak the Barbarian*: 'A smell of offal and garbage, sweet sputtering torch wood, strange drugs and incense, narrow thoroughfares that still stink in the crisp frosty air. A beggar blocks the narrow street.

'Just one dishna Outlander.'

'Stand out of my path.'

The mendicant glanced right and left as if seeking assistance. The narrow alley of shuttered shops was empty. Just ahead, where the street became a slop strewn stair half the level of a house, revellers could be seen on the upper levels. They raced back and forth across a square under the frosted blue light from torches set in the walls. It's all very Thief of Baghdad Adventure stories, evoking Audrey's fantasies of danger in far-away places. A bit tinsel and worn at the seams, the sky is thin as paper here. It's escape from the fever, from his corrupted flesh into a world of magic and adventure.

And here's *The Shootist* after a shootout: 'The bite of smoke was in his nose and the taste of death on his tongue the danger past and now the sweat and suddenly the nothingness, the sweet clean feel of being born.' Audrey could feel the custom made .44 in his hands, the short unsighted nickel-plated barrel, the pearl handle shimmering like a happy cloak, the smooth light double action, the deadly precision of bullets grouping within a two inch circle at 20 yards, the sweet clean feeling of being born without memory of the past.

In this quarter of vacant lots and rubbish a child sad as the death of monkeys offered us his pictures of a squirrel hunt (a shared interest in slightly dangerous sports . . . pistol licenses will be issued . . . I don't believe in miracles). I will be off with the wild geese in the sick smell of morning.

'The beggar raced towards the stairs shouting "Darters ho! A stranger down here in Sweetmeat Alley!" In the blowing murk a company of small lithe figures who had been racing past wheeled into sight. A dozen or more filthy boys screeched and squealed down the stairs. The boys formed a circle just up the street, dirty-skinned underfed waifs with pointed wolf's teeth they gave off a rank sharp animal smell. Where eye pits should have been, each carried two silver disks embedded between eyebrow and cheek bone. Their finger tips too were made of this silver crystal stuff and pointed like needles. A boy somewhat taller than the rest stepped forward. The blind crystal silver disks winked with reflections of the smoky blue torches round about. He capered in his animal skin breech clout and executed a contemptuous bow.'

Audrey decided that the Darter Boys were a noble invention like the Happy Cloak.

He turned back to *An Outcast of the Islands* and the superb description of Willem's corrupt infatuation for Aissa: 'From Willem's features the spark of reason vanished under her gaze and was replaced by an appearance of physical well being, an ecstacy of the senses that proclaimed its terrible work by an appalling aspect of idiotic beatitude. Then he whispered "I wish I could die like this now." That whisper of deadly happiness so sincere, so spontaneous, coming so straight from the heart like every corruption . . . It was the voice of madness, of happiness that is infamous, cowardly and so exquisite that the debased mind refuses to contemplate its termination or its price. His thoughts were so remote from her understanding that she let the words pass unnoticed like the breath of the wind like the flight of a cloud.'

Willem's corruption lies in his own white heart and soul. He is not like the victims of Circe enslaved by a potent and evil will. He is enslaved by his own passions and Aissa is drafted into a role she does not understand and does not want. It is Willems who carries with him all the gloomy Nordic myths, the Love Death, the Earth Mother who hangs her naked consort at the Spring Festival, The White Goddess eating her mate, Circe who turns men into swine. Not that he is conscious of all this being at once a very simple and a very corrupt man. He does not know that he is The Goat God who meets Crazy Aissa by the stream anymore than Almayer thinks of Circe when he urges his little daughter to call after Willems, 'Pig, Pig, Pig.'

Audrey closed his eyes and the story of Willems, Aissa, Almayer and Lingard unfolded, moving of its own volition, the sky, the river and the jungle in vivid colors, the white dim shadows in a grainy old film.

'The Darters' pointed teeth glittered. Others hopped from one dirty foot to the other hissing between their teeth. The silver crystal disks of their eyes shone with a strange luminescence as they shuffled forward in a closing semicircle.' Electric tremors run down Audrey's body and he comes out in a red rash that spreads into great red patches shivering, burning, now Jimmy has the fever too. Whistle on sweet young breath, a peal of clear laughter in the stirring grass leaving behind a faint scent of blossoms and an acrid smell of decay. Ether vertigo a whirling black funnel. Darkness blew in a whiff of brimstone.

'Up flew the hands of the Darter Boys. From the tips of their silver fingers light hissed through the air. Molten droplets pricked against his skin bringing exquisite agony with every contact. He raged and cursed swinging his sword into a firestorm of exploding sparks spurting from the needle fingers of the Darter Boys. Dimly he saw flashes of silver disk eyes through exploding patterns of light. He came to himself strapped to the reeking hide of a snow camel. Darter Boys ran alongside. They chittered and chirruped among themselves, their huge disk eyes turned up to catch the reflection of the lost mournful stars.'

Indistinct vision of a man going away from him diminishing in a long perspective of trees growing smaller but never going out of sight. 'Something familiar about that figure,' Willems thought, reminded him of something a long time ago . . . Why!! Himself!! And going away where?

Bugger the Queen

I guess you all read about the trouble the Sex Pistols had in England over their song 'God Save the Queen (It's a Fascist Regime)'. Johnny Rotten got hit with an iron bar wielded by HER Loyal Subjects. It's almost treason in England to say anything against what they call 'OUR Queen'. I don't think of Reagan as OUR President, do you? He's just the one we happen to be stuck with at the moment. So in memory of the years I spent in England — and in this connection I am reminded of a silly old Dwight Fisk song: 'Thank you a lot, Mrs Lousberry Goodberry, for an infinite weekend with you . . . (five years that weekend lasted) . . . For your cocktails that were hot and your baths that were not. . . so in fond memory of those five years I have composed this lyric which I hope someday someone will sing in England. It's entitled: *Bugger the Queen.*

My husband and I (The Queen always starts her spiel that way) / *The old school tie / Hyphenated names / Tired old games/It belongs in the bog* (Bog is punk for W.C.)/ *With the rest of the sog / Pull the chain on Buckingham / The drain calls you, MA'AM* (Have to call the Queen 'Ma'am' you know) / *BUGGER THE QUEEN!*

The audience takes up the refrain as they surge into the streets screaming 'BUGGER THE QUEEN'

Suddenly a retired major sticks his head out a window, showing his great yellow horse-teeth as he clips out: 'Buggah the Queen!'

A vast dam has broken.

It's like in Ireland, where they have a form of life known as Gombeen Man. Now a Gombeen Man is a blackmailer, police informer, receiver, money-lender. In small villages he often runs a shop and leans on the scale when he comes to the punch line. . .

'Well now Lord Brambletie I always say that what a gentlemen does in his own house is a gentleman's business, but there are those as thinks otherwise. . .'

(Lean . . . lean . . . lean . . .)

'Oh uh will you deliver that please?'

'Certainly sir. A pleasure sir.'

Arrives at the house...'Well Danny me lad, been out back of the spring house playing like a boy will, haven't you now?'

(Lean . . .lean . . .lean . . .)

And here's a woman having an affair with a tinker while her husband is doing a hitch in the Navy and due back on leave. . .word in his ear . . .and 'Well Mrs. O'Malley and top of the morning to you — Sure and your pots must need a sight of mending . . .and did you ever stop to ask yourself what the term a 'tinker's dame' signifies *Mrs. O'Malley*?' (Lean . . . lean . . . lean . . .)

Here is the Gombeen Man on a house call. Arrives all huffing and puffing and sits down without being asked.

'Ay and here's your steak Lord Brambletie, as fine a piece of meat as you've ever handled if you'll pardon the expression sir . . .Always glad to be of service to a gentleman and there's one way you can tell a *real* gentleman, a *real* gentleman isn't mean, and he doesn't give himself airs, like . . .I could do with a spot of something to keep out the cold. And you don't mind if I slip my shoes off do you, it's a long punishing walk out here from town and me feet is killing me. You wouldn't have a pad for me bunion would you me Lord?'

That's a Gombeen Man in action. Sure and he'll make Lord Brambletie put the pad to his corn with his very own lily whites and that's worth more to the Gombeen Man than a hundred pounds. A real Gombeen Man is in it more for the game than the money. He gets more satisfaction out of selling someone stew beef for top sirloin or shorting a sharp housewife a quarter pound than he would from a fat check handed him by a solicitor for some letters or photo negatives. He wants *contact* . . .

'Oh it's not money I'm after Lord Brambletie. Just dropped in for a little chat like . . .'

A word of advice to you young people: Always beware of a whore who says she doesn't want money. And a blackmailer who doesn't want money is the worst kind. He wants your blood, and like the whore who doesn't want money he'll get more money out of you in the end. Soon Lord Brambletie will pay him *anything* just to stay away.

A real Gombeen Man blackmails his victims by his very presence, his slimy, evil, insinuating presence. They don't watch him when he weighs a purchase because they don't want to be in contact with him.

203

Now English children are taught 'never to do anything you would be ashamed to do in front of the Queen' and that makes the Queen's picture blackmail right there. You see what we owe to George Washington and the Valley Forge boys for getting us out from under that blood-sucking picture. Imagine anyone telling his kids 'Don't do anything you'd be ashamed to do in front of President Reagan.' But for an Englishman, making it in front of the Queen's picture is like trying to have it off with a Gombeen Man at the foot of your bed . . .Don't mind me — like a spot of fun meself you know.'

And of course there are those as has a kinky thing with the Queen's picture. Either way, the Queen gets her tithe of flesh.

Now to come right out and say someone is a Gombeen Man is admitting you have something to hide, some reason you can be blackmailed, and so a good Gombeen Man may string it out for years before the moment of truth, when everybody looks into his neighbor's eyes and says . . .

'Did he lean on you?'

So then they all rise up and drive out the Gombeen Man.

Just as Pavlov's dogs salivated at the bell, that happy breed grovel in front of the Queen, indulging in that debased, degraded and downright disgusting English custom of 'knowing one's place', a custom enforced by an army of shopkeepers, waiters, hotel clerks and doormen.

Here's a young American with longish hair and some sort of musical instrument in a case, arriving in front of Brown's Hotel with his luggage and getting the old English treatment from the doorman.

Doorman, looking at the man's hair and the instrument case: 'Sorry sir, we're completely full sir.'

'But I called from the airport and made a reservation.'

'A mistake sir. Shall I call a cab sir? I'd suggest one of the larger places sir. More turnover you know.'

If he's got good sense he'll take that cab right back to the airport.

The Queen is the fountainhead and motherlode of a snobbery that poisons the dank air of England with the smell of brussels sprouts cooking in a soggy green paste. And what Englishman worthy of the name has not dreamed of being invited to Buckingham and having tea with the Queen, oh quite at ease you know. The Queen is leaning on every man woman and child in England. She's naught but a Gombeen Woman.

A vast crowd marches on Buckingham Palace screaming 'BUGGER THE QUEEN!'

Prince Philip comes out to say that after years of being the Royal Consort like a bloody stud horse, all he has to say is 'BUGGER THE QUEEN!'

It's like a re-make of the Magna Carta. Owing to a power shortage the Queen signs her abdication by flickering torch-light . . .and good riddance to the Gombeen Woman.